Building Bridges In A World Of Crumbling Connections

The Forgotten Calling That Belongs to All of Us

Ronald Higdon

Energion Publications
Gonzalez, FL
2022

Copyright @ 2022, Ronald Higdon

Unless otherwise indicated, Scripture quotations are taken from the Holy Bible, Today's New International Version, Copyright 2001, 2005 by International Bible Society. All rights reserved worldwide.

Scripture quotations marked BARCLAY are taken from The New Testament by William Barclay, copyright 1999 by Westminster John Knox Press, Louisville.

Scripture quotations marked BARNSTONE are taken from the Restored New Testament. New York: W. W. Norton & Company, 2009.

Scripture quotations marked HART are taken from The New Testament by David Bentley Hart, copyright 2017 by Yale University Press, New Haven.

Scripture quotations marked HOLMAN are taken from Holman Christian Standard Bible, copyright 2004 by Holman Bible Publishers, Nashville.

Scripture quotations marked LATTIMORE are taken from The New Testament translated by Richard Lattimore, copyright 1996 by the Bryn Mawr Trust Company. New York: North Point Press. All rights reserved.

Scripture quotations marked MESSAGE are taken from The Message. Copyright 1993, 1994, 1995, 2000, 2001. Used by permission of NavPress Publishing Group.

Scripture quotations marked MONTGOMERY are taken from The New Testament in Modern English translated by Helen Barrett Montgomery. Copyright 1924 by Judson Press, Valley Forge, Pa. First Holman Printing, 1988, used by permission.

Scripture quotations marked NEW are taken from A New New Testament edited by Hal Taussig, copyright 2013 by Houghton Mifflin Harcourt, Boston.

Scripture quotations marked NJB are taken from The New Jerusalem Bible, copyright 1985 by Darton, Longman & Todd, Ltd. and Doubleday Dell Publishing Group Inc. All rights reserved.

Scripture quotations marked NKJV are taken from The New King James Version, copyright 1979, 1980, 1982 by Thomas Nelson Inc., Nashville, Tennessee. All rights reserved.

Scripture quotations marked NLT are taken from the Holy Bible, New Living Translation, copyright 1996, 2004, 2007, 2013 by Tyndale House Foundation. Used by permission of Tyndale House Publishers, Inc., Carol Stream, Illinois 60188. All rights reserved.

Scripture quotations marked NRSV are taken from the New Revised Standard Version, copyright 1989 by the Division of Christian Education & the National Council of the Churches of Christ.

Scripture quotations marked PHILLIPS are taken from The New Testament in Modern English by J. B. Phillips, copyright 1968 by The Macmillan Company, New York.

Scripture quotations marked SCHONFIELD are taken from The Original New Testament by Hugh J. Schonfield, copyright 1998 by Element Books, Schafesbury, Dorset.

Scripture quotations marked WUEST are taken from The New Testament: An Expanded Translation by Kenneth S. Wuest, copyright 1961 by William B. Eerdmans Publishing Co., Grand Rapids.

ISBN: 978-1-63199-790-7
eISBN: 978-1-63199-791-4
Library of Congress Control Number: 2022939246

Energion Publications — P.O. Box 841 — Gonzalez, FL 32560
850-5350-3916
Energion.com — pubs@energion.com

TABLE OF CONTENTS

Preface	Moving From "Me" to "We"	v
Prefatory Introduction	Building Bridges in a World of Pluralization	ix
	The Big Picture: Many Cannot See The Forest For The Trees	1
1	Asking The Real Question: "Are You Reconciled?"	7
2	Living The Called Life	15
3	Creating Bridges Of Possibility	23
4	Forgiving & Accepting As We Have Been Forgiven & Accepted	33
5	Refusing To Make Our Ways And Standards Universal	43
6	Being Willing To Learn From Others	53
7	Giving Up The Joys Of Judgment	63
8	Placing The Emphasis On Actions Rather Than Emotions	73
9	Acknowledging No Limits To God's Love And Grace	83
10	Keeping Faith In The God Of Possibilities And Surprises	91
Conclusion	The Great And Final Reconciliation	105
	Bibliography Of Quoted Sources	107

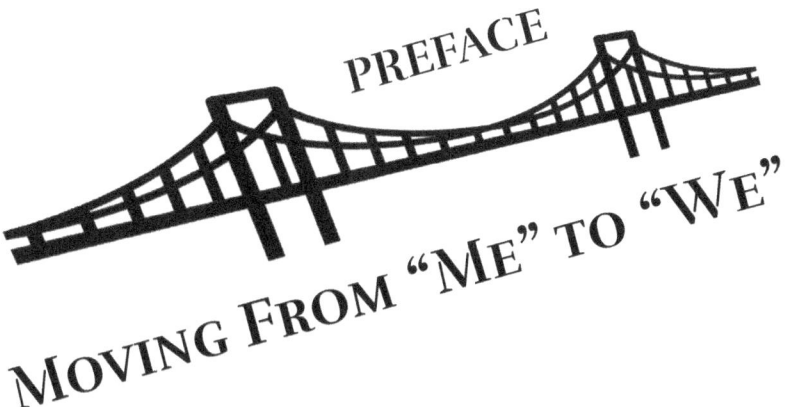

PREFACE
Moving From "Me" to "We"

Our culture seems to be marked in almost every way possible into two divisions: them and us. Boundaries are erected that separate us from those not like us in some particular way. To different degrees and for various reasons, we appear to have adopted one of the prayers in Jesus' parable in Luke 18:9-14 about two men who went to the Temple to pray. The proud Pharisee stood by himself and prayed this prayer: *"I thank you, God, that I am not a sinner like everyone else, especially like that tax collector over there!"* (18:11; NLT).

We are meant to see the Pharisee's apartness and his designation of another as unacceptable. To many in that day, his distance and his judgment might have seemed appropriate in the face of the tax collector's cooperation with the Roman conquerors. Many would have given a hearty "Amen" to the justifiable stance of the man who took his religion and his patriotism seriously. Although Jesus did not honor that separation or that judgment (he even chose a tax collector as one of his disciples), the common sense of the day accepted the "them" and "us" as a given in that situation. Jesus' assertion in teaching and action, as well as the totality of the biblical witness, maintains that there is only WE.

I find it significant that both the Declaration of Independence and the Constitution of the United States are "we" oriented. The

Constitution's beginning words speak of unity: "We the people of the United States…" The Declaration of Independence, after laying out the nature of the document, asserts: "We hold these truths to be self-evident.…" Sadly, it has taken many generations for these two "we's" to move beyond white males. In spite of its limitations, both documents emphasize a collective spirit, a mutual dedication, and cooperation, a strong sense of being in this thing together. I find nothing that would even hint at the hyper-individualism and the disregard of freedom as a word that takes for granted the individual as part of the community. Both documents would suggest that "we have our rights" is more appropriate than "I have my rights." They were "we" documents" from beginning to end.

The tragedy of our modern era is that politics is one of the major divisions; the "them" and "us" are major demarcations of the acceptable and the unacceptable. It is almost impossible to have a civil, intelligent, and sane discussion across party lines. The distance "across the aisle" in our chambers of government is at times beyond the range of human vision; the "others" are not even in sight. Add to this the racial, cultural, social, religious, educational, financial, and gender divisions, and we wonder where we can possibly begin to build bridges in this crumbling world of connections. I believe there is a place to begin and there is a way to begin. That's what this book is all about. We will journey through ten biblical challenges to building bridges in a world of crumbling connections. This does not mean in the world at large but in our world: family, friends, neighbors, associates at work, those in our religious community, those in the organizations to which we belong, those miscellaneous "strangers" we bump into as we go about our daily lives, those we might call our adversaries, and those we unfortunately might label "enemies."

A WORD ABOUT CHAPTER STRUCTURE

Each chapter is divided into three sections: Biblical Soundings, Ramifications, and Concluding Thoughts. In the first section, I attempt to bring the totality of the biblical witness to each text. No single verse of Scripture can be interpreted in isolation. There are always other considerations: "on the other hand…"; "in addition to this…"; "a seemingly contrary idea is…"; and "a wider view enables us to see that…." In Ramifications, I attempt to suggest parallel and related themes that can be developed from the cited texts. In Concluding Thoughts, I endeavor to bring the first two sections together while leaving open the door for further reflection and study. In biblical studies, these two ingredients are always necessary; there is never a final word, only a "with our best efforts while attempting to be open to the guidance of the Spirit and diligent study, our present understanding is…." As with almost everything in life, we must post at the end of our efforts: "To be continued."

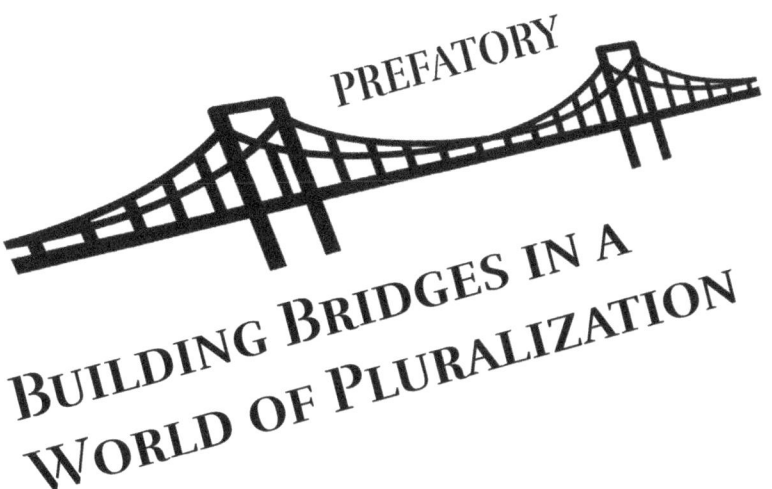

Prefatory
Building Bridges in a World of Pluralization

I didn't want to title this "Preface 2," so I chose "Prefatory," meaning, among other things: "preparatory" remarks. The world and culture in which we live is one unknown to any other generation. Two quick examples:

In this morning's Louisville Courier-Journal (October 14, 2021), an Associated Press article has this paragraph: "Vague, familiar-looking 'friend of a friend' stories are a dangerous form of misinformation because they 'feel like insider information being shared by individuals directly involved in the action,' according to Rachel Moran, a misinformation scholar at the University of Washington." (I withhold the article's title to protect the "guilty" and myself!). My comment: Whoever thought we would need misinformation scholars?!

Also in this morning's paper is this Pearl's Before Swine comic strip: In the first frame there is the statement: "Life's Motto From Birth to 2019" with a figure saying: "This too shall pass!" In frame two is the statement: "Life's Motto in 2020" with a figure saying, "This will probably pass." In the third frame, the statement is: "Life's Motto in 2021" with a figure saying: "What in the (blankety-blank) is happening?" In the last frame, Goat says, "I sense a downward trend," and Rat responds: "I fear next year's."

In one of my other books, *All I Need to Know I'm Still Learning at 80*, the first chapter is titled "There Are No Trains to Yesterday." It begins with a question from Eric Weiner: "Is there any moment other than the present?"[1] My next sentence is: "After the death of our older bipolar son to suicide in 2013, my wife and I found ourselves in line with countless others at the Regret station waiting for the "If Only" express."[2] Of course, the train never came; neither did the Zip-Express to the future. Life had to be lived exactly where we were as it opened daily into the present.

Difficult times make us long for other times when things were easier, although they usually were not as golden as we remember. The major challenge of life is to live when and where we are and face realistically and courageously the challenges that our current situation offers. This is where faith and perseverance become two of our watchwords. We're stuck with the present and that is where God expects us to live; there is no other option.

No other age has ever experienced the pluralization that now engulfs us in our culture. Os Guinness wrote in 1983 what is now true ten times over:

> Life is now a smorgasbord with an endless array of options. Whether a hobby, holiday, lifestyle, world-view, or religion, there's something for everybody…. Putting it simply, we have reached the stage in pluralization where choice is not just a state of affairs, it is a state of mind.…Change becomes the very essence of existence.[3]

Two problems immediately surface. The first is noted by Peter Berger in his book *The Heretical Imperative* where:

---

1   Eric Weiner, *Man Seeks God* (New York: Twelve, 2011), 216.
2   Ronald Higdon, *All I Need to Know I'm Still Learning at 80* (Gonzalez, FL: Energion Publications, 2017), 1.
3   William Raeper & Linda Edwards, *Brief Guide to Ideas* (Grand Rapids: Zondervan, 1997), 270.

"...he argued that in modern Western culture we are all required to be heretics when it comes to religion. Heresy means making an individual decision about matters of faith, over and against the given tradition of church or society.... To be respectable, you have to be a heretic, to make your own decisions about what to believe. There is now no such thing as orthodoxy in the old sense of the word, meaning to hold correct or currently accepted opinions on religious doctrine."[4]

The authors of the book from which that quote is taken then add: "On this view the principle of pluralism is overwhelmingly strong.... Lots of different truths exist side by side. The result is that religion becomes relativized. Truth is true if it's true for you. A different truth is true if it's true for me."[5] Pilate would feel right at home today with his question, "What is truth?" (John 18:38). In building bridges, I am not suggesting that everything must become relative and that we abandon our faith. The following chapters attempt to present ways in which we can establish positive relationships with others without giving up our faith or asking others to do the same. I feel like Billy Graham, who responded to the question of how he related to persons of other faiths: "I only have one story to tell. I leave everything else in God's hands."

The fear, anger, rage, and violence that fill our culture demand that we find ways to build community and live constructively with each other – in spite of our differences. Building bridges of reconciliation may open the door to sharing our faith on a different level, but, right now, to keep this world from blowing apart, we need to repair the crumbling connections. Following the destruction of the Temple and the city of Jerusalem, many of the Hebrews found themselves in Babylon. They asked a logical question: *"How can we sing the songs of the Lord while in a foreign land?"* (Psalm 137:4). They may not have liked Jeremiah's answer to their question, but

---

4   Ibid, 272.
5   Ibid.

it was the only possible answer. Here is part of a letter he wrote to the exiles in Babylon:

Thus says the Lord of hosts, the God of Israel to all the exiles whom I have sent into exile from Jerusalem to Babylon: Build houses and live in them, plant gardens and eat what they produce. Take wives and have sons and daughters there and do not decrease. But seek the welfare of the city where I have sent you into exile and pray to the Lord on its behalf, for in its welfare you will find your welfare. (Jeremiah 29:4-7).

My paraphrase of God's prescription for the exiles: "Invest yourselves fully in life where you are and as it is right now. Don't hold back. Give it all you've got. You've spent enough time lamenting, now get rid of your self-pity and resentment. Be model citizens in this foreign land and make it a better place for your being there." This sounds very much like Jesus' Sermon on the Mount, where he tells his followers how to live in their difficult time: a time of Roman occupation, heavy taxation, and unfilled messianic expectations. They are to love their enemies (the Romans), turn the other cheek, go the second mile, be the salt of the earth and the light of the world, not worry and trust that God will provide for them (Matthew 5 – 7).

No hunkering down in either of these. Not a single idea of just getting through the difficult times but of really living in the difficult times (which often feels like living in a foreign land). They were not asked to destroy relationships and blow-up bridges. Just like them, we are being asked to be God's people and carry out our calling in this challenging and demanding age which, like all other ages, is full of amazing possibilities.

INTRODUCTION

THE BIG PICTURE:
MANY CANNOT SEE THE FOREST FOR THE TREES

It is regrettable that we no longer "hear" the biblical message as the original "listeners" did. In an oral world of very low literacy, readers were those who enabled even the most uneducated to receive the message. The Scriptures were meant to be heard. That hearing has the distinct advantage of getting across the big picture. When I heard the gospel of Mark recited in its entirety by a professor, it was like hearing it for the first time. The impact was of the Gospel in its entirety. My question is always: when you take a Gospel as a single unit (no chapters or verses, which, of course, were not part of the original), what do you hear? What is the central message? What are the major emphases? What is the big picture?

In my youthful days of yearly two-week revivals, that big picture often got lost in the almost exclusive emphasis on personal salvation. "Are you saved?" was the keynote of evangelistic preaching, often with the addendum, "Are you sure?" Walking the aisle (or the earlier "sawdust trail" in tent revivals), followed by a personal confession of faith, "sealed the deal." The transaction was complete and our names were recorded in "The Lamb's Book of Life" (Revelation 21:27) which no one and no power could ever erase. That was known as the "eternal security of the believer" or, more commonly, "once saved, always saved."

I have never doubted that "conversion" involves a decision on our part. In my tradition, it means somewhere along the way and in some manner, we must respond with a "Yes" to what we perceive as Jesus' invitation: "Follow me" (which biblically appears to be the only one he ever gave). I remember reading somewhere that Catherine Marshall described it as God's finding the secret stairway into each person's heart. The mystery of the working of God's Spirit in the hearts and lives of people is much too complex to be reduced to any simple, mechanical formula accompanied by several stanzas of "Just As I Am." Biblically, it is the beginning of an acknowledged relationship with the Creator and Sustainer of life. It is to enter into a very special "covenant relationship."

Much has been lost because too many have forgotten the original designations for the Hebrew and Christian Scriptures. Willis Barnstone writes in the forward to his translation: "New Covenant is an exact translation of the Greek *kaine diatheke* found in the Septuagint and in Paul's 1 Corinthians 11:25 and Hebrews 8:8-13. The title New Testament derives from *Novum Testamentum*, a mistranslation appearing in the Vulgate, the fourth-century Latin translation attributed to Jerome....New Covenant is the preferred title and presented (as here on the title page) as "The New Covenant, commonly called The New Testament."[1]

> We first encounter the actual Greek words "new covenant" (not "new testament") in Paul: *"Our competence is from God, who has made us competent to be ministers of a new covenant, not of letter but of spirit, for the letter kills, but the Spirit gives life"* (2 Corinthians 3:6)....In no place in his letters did Paul call for new scriptures to be assembled into a Christian Bible. As a Jew who died before the gospels were composed, who sought to convince coreligionists that Yeshua was the messiah, Paul would scarcely have foreseen a new compendium of holy scripture that might be added to or replace the long-since canonized Hebrew Bible. It was the Church Fathers Tertullian

---

1 Willis Barnstone, *The New Covenant*, Vol 1 (New York: Riverhead Books, 2002), 9.

(ca. 160-230) and Origen (ca. 185-254) who were among the first to use the term "Old Covenant" for the Hebrew Bible."[2]

This additional section from the same article provides an insight that many are unaware of. (It is why I continue to use the term "Hebrew Scriptures").

> Hebrew names for the Bible are Torah (meaning "law" or "instruction") or Tanak (an acronym from initial Hebrew letters for Torah, Prophets, and Writings), or the three major divisions of Tanak: Torah (Five Books of Moses) Nevi'im (Prophets), and Kethuvim (Writings). Whatever name is given by Jews to the Bible it is not properly the old, nor the testament, nor the covenant.[3]

Barnstone later issued the complete New Testament under the title of *Restored New Testament* (Subtitle: A New Translation with Commentary, Including the Gnostic Gospels Thomas, Mary, and Judas). This is one of my "must" recommendations, not only for the excellent translation and copious footnotes, but also for almost 300 pages of informative and provocative articles. The cover overleaf gives reasons for this being "a magnificent biblical translation for our age":[4]

> For the first time since the King James Version in 1611, Willis Barnstone has given us an amazing literary and historical version of the New Testament. Barnstone preserves the original song of the Bible, rendering a large part in poetry and the epic Revelation in incantatory blank verse. This monumental translation is the first to restore the original Greek, Aramaic, and Hebrew names (Markos for Mark, Yeshua for Jesus), thereby revealing the Greco-Jewish identity of biblical people and places. Citing historical and biblical scholarship, he changes the sequence of texts and adds three seminal Gnostic gospels. Each book has elegant introductions and is thoroughly annotated.

---

2   Ibid, 514.
3   Ibid, 515
4   Willis Barnstone, *Restored New Testament* (New York: W. W. Norton & Company, 2009), cover overleaf.

GOD IS A COVENANT-MAKING GOD FROM THE BEGINNING

The God of biblical revelation is a God-in-relationship. That is why you find the word covenant so early in the pages of Scripture. "The major covenants in the Hebrew Bible between God and Israel and the patriarchs are through Noah (Genesis 9:9), Abraham (15:18), Moses (Exodus 19:5, 24.7), and David (2 Samuel 7.14). In the New Testament, there are covenants in Matthew 26.28; Mark 14.24: , 87.8-13, 9.15, and 12.24; 1 Corinthians 11.25; and Hebrews 7.22."[5] The God who speaks to Moses from the burning bush identifies himself in relational terms: *I am the God of your father, the God of Abraham, the God of Isaac, the God of Jacob* (Exodus 3:6). Moses is instructed to assemble the elders of Israel (in Egypt) and tell them: "*The Lord, the God of your ancestors, the God of Abraham, of Isaac, and the God of Jacob, has sent me to you*" (Exodus 3:16).

In the history of early religions, this is unprecedented. The Israelites are not going to have to get God's attention, they already have it. This God is the one who makes pledges from the beginning. Following the flood, the words to Noah are: *I am establishing my covenant with you and your descendants after you, and with every living creature. ....Never again shall all flesh be cut off by the waters of a flood....This is the sign of the covenant that I make between me and every living creature that is with you, for all future generations: I have set my bow in the clouds, and it shall be a sign of the covenant between me and the earth* (Genesis 9:12-13). This covenant with all creation is followed by the covenant with Abraham and his descendants (Genesis 17). This covenant is larger than Abraham ever could have imagined. An angel of the Lord brings this message following the "binding of Isaac": *by your offspring shall all the nations of the earth gain blessing for themselves*" (Genesis 22:18).

The God of Scripture is a covenant-making, promise-making, commitment-making God. All of this at his initiative. All of this is based, not on who we are, but on who he is. Psalm 115:1 gives a theme that is echoed many times in this hymnbook: *Not to us,*

---

5   Ibid, 199.

O Lord, not to us, but to your name give glory, for the sake of your steadfast love and your faithfulness. God's love and faithfulness undergird all of his covenants; God's love and faithfulness undergird his world.

THE BIG PICTURE OF A SEARCHING GOD

The Bible is not the story of people who "found" God and with instructions on how we can find him. The underlying thesis is that God is not the one in hiding, we are. In Genesis 3, we do not find Adam and Eve searching for God after the rupture in their relationship with him. They are in hiding and we have the picture of God walking in the Garden in the cool of the day (3:8), calling out, "Where are you?" That remains the classic question of all Scripture; it is not "Where is God?" but "Where are we?" The biblical witness tells us of the searching God who keeps calling and inviting and imploring us to come out of hiding. In the history of religion, this kind of a god is unheard of. Rachel Held Evans captures this "seeking" God in these words:

> …the God of Scripture stoops and stoops and stoops. At the heart of the gospel message is the story of a God who stoops to the point of death on a cross. Dignified or not, believable or not, ours is a God perpetually on bended knee, doing everything it takes to convince stubborn and petulant children that they are seen and loved.[6]

The purpose of all this searching and stooping is to restore the relationship with his creation. It is easy to get lost in the splendor of the New Jerusalem and the blessings of life in the restored Eden in the book of Revelation. The real miracle of the next life and the greatest blessing of all is the end of hiding and separation in the restored relationship described in Revelation 21:3 – *And I heard a loud voice from the throne saying, "Look! God's dwelling place is now among the people, and he will dwell with them. They will be his people,*

---

6   Rachel Held Evans, Inspired (New York: Nelson Books, 2018), 12.

and God himself will be with them and be their God. Reconciliation and bridge-building have now achieved their purpose.

What Counts The Most.

There will be many specifics in the chapters that follow but I firmly believe that what is most important has been captured in a book I read many years ago, marked with five stars and wrote "Yes!" in the margin:

> Life is not a programmed tape in some celestial computer, with our life assignment to develop the keypunch skills necessary to retrieve the predetermined decisions made for us by the Divine Programmer. God does have some very concrete purposes for us: that we grow in God's image, that we avoid mutilating the design. But in the majority of decisions we make in life, God seems more interested in the context of our choice than in the content. It matters more to God that we choose and how we choose than what we choose. In other words, as long as the context of our decision is informed, reconciling, compassionate, and impassioned, one decision is often as good as another. This is the meaning of Augustine's famous dictum, "Love God and do what you will."[7]

---

[7] Leonard I. Sweet, *New Life in the Spirit* (Philadelphia: The Westminster Press, 1982), 71.

ASKING THE REAL QUESTION: "ARE YOU RECONCILED?"

BIBLICAL SOUNDINGS

2 Corinthians 5:18-6:1 — *All this is from God, who reconciled us to himself through Christ and gave us the ministry of reconciliation; that God was reconciling the world to himself in Christ, not counting people's sins against them. And he has committed to us the message of reconciliation. We are therefore Christ's ambassadors, as though God were making his appeal through us. We implore you on Christ's behalf: Be reconciled to God. God made him who had no sin to be sin for us, so that in him we might become the righteousness of God. As God's co-workers we urge you not to receive God's grace in vain.*

AN ENGLISH WORD THAT IS NOT BIG ENOUGH

My adolescent days are filled with memories of the annual "Revival" and a guest evangelist whose dynamic, enthusiastic, and dramatic presentation of the gospel along with "special music" rivaled any entertainment venue being offered. It usually resulted in "packed pews." (I use that term because there was ordinarily a "pact the pew" night with some kind of reward for those who were able to do so.) For a week or two, it was the best show in town.

The goal was to get as many people as possible "saved." At the conclusion of each service, there was an "invitation" hymn; people were invited to come forward, confess their faith in Christ as savior, and become a candidate for baptism. It was usually quite protracted with "Just As I Am," or some appropriate hymn, being sung a number of times, depending on how the evangelist perceived the "moving of the Spirit."

Our "regular" church services seemed quite tame after the "spectacular, spectacular" of the revival ended its run. I do not doubt that many had significant changes brought about in their lives as a result of some decision made during the event. I do not doubt the sincerity or best intentions of most of those involved. What began to bother me and caused me to do some soul (and biblical) searching was that "You need to get saved" just didn't seem to be a big enough phrase to capture the dramatic reorientation of life called for in the preaching of John and Jesus with their cry: "Repent!" The basic meaning of the Greek word metanoia is a change of mind.

Both the baptizer in the wilderness and the prophet from Nazareth began their ministries with the same invitation: *After John was put in prison, Jesus went into Galilee, proclaiming the good news of God. "The time has come," he said. "The kingdom of God has come near. Repent and believe the good news"* (Mark 1:14-15). This was a call to put on Kingdom glasses and see the world and one's life from an entirely different perspective. It was a call for the kind of living described in the Sermon on the Mount (Matthew 5-7). It was a call to be "born from above" (John 3). I contend this is a more accurate translation than the usual "born again" which even Nicodemus couldn't understand! Jesus' invitation, "Follow me," is basically the only one he ever gave. And, as radical as it sounds, in what we call the Great Commission (Matthew 28:19-2), Jesus did not command his followers to get people saved. His one command was: make disciples! "Are you saved?" isn't a big enough question to begin to encompass what Jesus meant when he described his followers as the salt of the earth and the light of the world (Matthew 5:13-16).

GOD, IN CHRIST, WAS IN THE RECONCILING BUSINESS

The casual reader of most English translations of the New Testament might justifiably assume that Jesus Christ is the full name of Jesus of Nazareth. "Christ" is a title and not a name. The best translation is "Jesus the Anointed One" which designates him as the long-awaited Messiah. (2 Corinthians 5:18, NEW). The ultimate and final seeking by God to reconcile his creation to himself was accomplished in sending his Son to *"pitch his tent among us"* (the literal rendering of John 1:14). I have always liked what Eugene Peterson did with this verse in his paraphrasing translation, *The Word became flesh and blood, and moved into the neighborhood* (MESSAGE). This is God's person-to-person move in his ultimate revelation (Hebrews 1:1-3) and the final step in his means and method of reconciliation.

God's purpose from Genesis to Revelation is plainly to break down the barriers that separate us from him and from one another. Galatians 3:26-28 announces the results of God's reconciling efforts: *So in Christ Jesus you are all children of God through faith, for all of you who were baptized into Christ have clothed yourselves with Christ. There is neither Jew nor Gentile, neither slave nor free, neither male nor female, for you are all one in Christ Jesus. If you belong to Christ, then you are Abraham's seed, and heirs according to the promise.* When you read these verses keep the title designation clear*: So in Messiah Jesus you are all children of God through faith.... The Message* puts verse 26 this way*: In Christ's family there can be no division....*

God's reconciling work began with the call to Abraham. His initiative in that call is followed by his continuing initiatives throughout Hebrew Scripture. After using a bowl of stew to purchase Esau's birthright and deceiving his aged father, Isaac, with his mother's devious planning, receives the family blessing, and finds himself on the run as a result of his brother's death threat. At this moment, he hardly appears to be the likely candidate for the designated Abrahamic covenant bearer. When Jacob stops for a night's rest, he sleeps on a rock-pillow and has a dream. (Note: in Scripture, dreams are clearly accepted as one of the major ways God communicates.) He dreams of a ladder extending from earth to heaven with the angels of God ascending and descending. (The order of their movement is no minor notation.) *There above it stood the Lord, and he said: "I am the Lord, the God of your father Abraham and the God of Isaac....All peoples on earth will be blessed through you and your offspring....I am with you and will watch over you wherever you go, and I will bring you back to this land. I will not leave you until I have done what I have promised you* (Genesis 28:10-15).

Jacob's response to his dream has become a classic line: *Surely the Lord is in this place – and I did not know it!"* (Genesis 28:16). Even with his treachery, deceit, and resulting speedy exit, he had not outdistanced God. He had not stepped beyond the boundaries of God's reconciling grace. He had not left God back home with the family and city (many of the gods worshipped in that day were local deities). It was not only surprising that God was in this place but there was additionally the surprising pledge from God to always be where Jacob is and to work with him to keep the promised blessing operative. My take: we never have to catch up with God; he always catches up with us – wherever and however we are. We will never find ourselves in a place God has vacated. No wonder Jacob's next response following the recognition of God's presence seems entirely appropriate: And he was afraid, and said, *"How awesome is this place! This is none other than the house of God, and this is the gate of heaven"* (Genesis 28:17).

If we are now Abraham's seed and heirs according to the promise, it should not be unusual for us to realize on many occasions: *How awesome is this place! This is none other than the house of God, and this is the gate of heaven.* Perhaps, as it did for Jacob, something like this is more likely to occur when we have a rock for a pillow and are on the run from something that threatens to destroy us.

Our reconciling God appears to have some special "blessing places" and this appears to be one of his favorites.

Ramifications

Do You Need A "Point Of Faith Shower Cap"?

About the time you think you have seen about everything in the "religion business," something comes along that lets you know market ingenuity knows no bounds. Years ago, this something came in a letter a friend of mine received. It was a form letter in which his name had been inserted by a computer program to make it "personal." The letter was from Rev. _____, pastor of the "Church by Mail." In part, the letter read: "I really believe you are under some kind of heavy load. But, I know that God showed me how I am to help you get rid of it. A few days ago I was in my hotel room…and while standing in front of the mirror, my attention was drawn to the shower cap laying on the sink. I felt impressed to hold it in my hands. When I picked it up, the scripture of St. Mark 16:18 "…*they shall lay HANDS on the sick, and they shall recover,*" came to my mind. Then, I thought of you and I knew what the Lord wanted me to do with the shower cap. The Holy Spirit led me to trace my right hand on the shower cap and mail the shower cap to you."

A piece of folded paper was enclosed which was headed: "IMPORTANT INSTRUCTIONS TO YOU ON THIS POINT OF FAITH SHOWERCAP":

1. You don't have to put it on. Just touch it to your head. If you do put it on, keep it on for only 7 minutes – no longer than 7 minutes. 7 is God's perfect number (Genesis 2:3).
2. Do not take a shower in this shower cap, and do not get it wet. Please: this is spiritual.
3. Nicely, fold it back up and place it back in this little plastic bag. Then place it in the enclosed envelope addressed to me.

4. Put your offering in this enclosed envelope, "NOT IN THE SHOWERCAP."

When I completed my reading, I couldn't decide whether to laugh or cry. Perhaps if one is desperate enough, the possibility of using God's perfect number 7 (biblically it has to do with completeness, wholeness) to obtain healing for some heavy load might not seem so outrageous after all. Many have believed that some special offering, a special pilgrimage, a special prayer, or some special ritual might persuade God to make his healing and redemptive move. None ever saw this as forcing God's hand, but for all practical purposes, this was the intention. If putting on a shower cap for 7 minutes could get God's attention, why not give it a try? What harm could be done by wearing a spiritual shower cap for seven minutes a day? My answer: a lot!

At no time did the Hebrew Scriptures suggest that any kind of ritual or offering would work magic. Nothing "works" apart from our relationship with God and one another. Jesus clearly spells this out when he is asked which is the greatest commandment in the law. He replies, "*'Love the Lord your God with all your heart and with all your soul and with all your mind.' This is the first and greatest commandment. And the second is like it: 'Love your neighbor as yourself.' All the Law and the Prophets hand on these two commandments*" (Matthew 22:37-40).

An illustration of this principle is revealed in Jesus' parable of the two men who go to the temple to pray. One stands by himself (important to note!) and thanks God he is not like other people – *robbers, evildoers, adulterers – or even like this tax collector.* He then reminds God that he fasts twice a week and gives a tenth of all he receives. The other man stood at a distance, refused to look up to heaven, and voiced his single sentence prayer, "*God, have mercy on me a sinner*" (Luke 18:9-14). When Jesus announces that this was the person who went home *justified before God*, it was a shocking revelation to his audience. This tax collector was in a right relationship with God and the Pharisee was not; what separated the Pharisee from his fellow pray-er also separated him from God.

WHAT IS THE GOSPEL ABOUT, ANYWAY?

A cartoon appeared in the Wall Street Journal picturing a prophet carrying a sign that reads: REPENT! Below in smaller writing it states: "If you have already repented, disregard this notice." Although there is no record of anyone carrying such a sign in Philippi, that message appears to have been accepted by some in the church. They had repented, been converted, been baptized, and saw their faith as a completed transaction. So, Paul has to say to these people whom he dearly loves: *God who began a good work in you will carry it on to completion…(so) continue to work out your salvation with fear and trembling* (Philippians 1:6; 2:12). What needs to be addressed? Relationships! *"I plead with Euodia and I plead with Syntyche to be of the same mind the Lord"* (4:2). Being in a right relationship with one another is one of the dimensions in working out our salvation with fear and trembling.

> Elsewhere in these letters (to his son) I write about how I became a Christian when I was fifteen years old. It's strange the way we Christians usually speak about becoming a Christian as though it were something we did once and were done with, like getting our tonsils taken out. In reality, accepting Jesus as Lord and Savior is just the first and easiest part of the lifelong task of becoming a Christian.[1]

The initial reconciliation with God, others, and ourselves needs daily reconnection. "The essential function of religion is to radically connect us with everything. (Religio = to re-ligament or reconnect)."[2] The Pharisee who stands by himself as he prays at the temple does not realize that this "apartness" is his basic problem. The fragmentation of our present culture is exactly what the gos-

---

1 Tony and Bart Campolo, *Things We Wish We Had Said* (Dallas: Word Incorporated, 1989), 98.
2 Richard Rohr, *The Universal Christ* (New York: Convergent, 2019), 7.

pel is meant to address. Like the Pharisee, too many believe that holding the right political or cultural position on issues places them on a superior plane and rightly distances them from those who the unworthy (other much harsher and more judgmental adjectives are often). Perhaps the *fear and trembling* part comes in when we realize how difficult it is to be reconciled to those who certainly do not appear to be "like us." Our "more righteous than others" attitude is the very thing for which Jesus condemned some of the Pharisees.

"What did Jesus teach? He had no system, no summa, no code. God forbid! The only way to grasp his teaching is to read all the Gospels repeatedly until its essence permeates the mind."[3] When I attempt this kind of perspective on the gospel Jesus presented, I know some of that fear and trembling Paul talks about. The big picture of solid, healthy, caring, forgiving, and redemptive relationships in all areas of life reminds me of just how much work remains to be done in the working out of my salvation. Campolo is right. Becoming a Christian is indeed a lifelong task.

Concluding Thoughts

A "bumper sticker" faith with snappy slogans and pithy quips of complex theological concepts, reduces the biblical faith to an unrecognizable simplicity. The searching God of the Scriptures and the relational nature of the covenants (both Hebrew and Christian) make both the demands and questions of faith too comprehensive for any kind of reduction to a simple one-time transaction. Reconciliation is always a work in progress.

---

3   Paul Johnson, *Jesus: A Biography from a Believer* (New York: Viking, 2010), 82.

LIVING THE CALLED LIFE

BIBLICAL SOUNDINGS

2 Corinthians 5:18-20; 6:1 (LATTIMORE) — *So that one who is in Christ is a new creature; the old is gone, behold, the new is here; and all is from God, who reconciled us with himself through Christ and gave us this ministry of reconciliation....So we are ambassadors for Christ, as if God were summoning you through us....Working with him, we implore you not to let God's grace be given in vain.*

IS THIS THE FORGOTTEN CALLING?

No one has ever written that the "Great Commission" of Matthew 28:19-20 was given only to the current disciples or was intended only for "professional" religious workers. It has always been understood as being for all of Jesus' followers. No one believes that when Jesus said, *My commandment is this: Love each other as I have loved you* (John 15:12), he meant it only for those in the Upper Room with him. Why has this not also been true of the ministry of reconciliation? Frequently, chapter and verse divisions separate items that can only be understood as a continuous flow of ideas. These markers were intended to make it easier to locate the ideas in

Scripture; they were never intended to be seen as division markers. 2 Corinthians 6:1 flows immediately from the ideas in verses 17 through 21. It reads: *As we work together with him, we urge you also not to accept the grace of God in vain.*

Other translations of 2 Corinthians 6:1 spell out this implication that the calling to the ministry of reconciliation is the universal calling for all of Jesus' disciples: *As God's co-workers we urge you not to receive God's grace in vain* (TNIV); *Companions are we are in this work with you, we beg you, please don't squander one bit of this marvelous life God has given us* (MESSAGE); *Therefore, as God's fellow workers, we also appeal to you not to receive his loving kindness in vain* (NEW); *As cooperators with God himself we beg you, then, not to fail to use the grace of God* (PHILLIPS). Case closed!

It Begins Where We Are With The People We Know

Therefore, if you are offering your gift at the altar and there remember that your brother or sister has something against you, leave your gift there in front of the altar. First go and be reconciled to that person; then come and offer your gift (Matthew 5:23-24).

Here is one of the many verses in Scripture where the principle is intended and not the literal application. Many commentators note that it would be impossible to leave an offering unattended; the principle is all too clear and the context is provided by William Barclay (although it lacks the gender inclusiveness of our time):

> To be effective, sacrifice had to include confession of sin and true penitence; and true penitence involved the attempt to rectify any consequences sin might have had. The great Day of Atonement was held to make atonement for the sins of the whole nation, but the Jews were quite clear that not even the sacrifices of the Day of Atonement could avail for a man unless he was first reconciled to his neighbor. The breach between man and God could not be healed until the breach between man and man was healed.[1]

---

1 William Barclay, *The Daily Study Bible: The Gospel of Matthew*, Vol 1 (Philadelphia: The Westminster Press, 1958), 139

Nowhere in Scripture is reconciliation a strictly private and personal affair between the individual and God. It always involves others and is also most frequently in the context of community. It is impossible to be "right" with God without first attempting to be "right" with others. When Jesus was asked which was the greatest commandment in the Law, he combined Deuteronomy 6:5 and Leviticus 19:18: *"'Love the Lord your God with all your heart, and with all your soul and with all your mind.' This is the first and greatest commandment. And the second is like it: 'Love your neighbor as yourself.' All the Law and the Prophets hang on these two commandments"* (Matthew 22:37-40).

Cain was never going to be right with God and his offering was never going to be acceptable because he was not right with his brother (Genesis 4:1-16). Many have told me they thought it was unfair that God never told Cain what was wrong with his offering. I believe the text does tell us: *The Lord looked with favor on Abel and his offering, but on Cain and his offering he did not look with favor* (Genesis 4:4-5). There is no evidence to suggest that any regulations had been established concerning acceptable or unacceptable offerings. There was nothing wrong with Cain's offering; he was a farmer and offered a produce offering. There was a great deal wrong with Cain. It appears to be the classic sibling rivalry, the details of which are omitted. We do get indications of the problem when we are told that Cain *was very angry* (vs. 5) and when God tells him that *sin is crouching at your door* (vs. 7).

What makes the ministry of reconciliation so challenging is that it begins with our own families and is meant to extend to all of those who make up our neighborhood of relationships. This is quite a calling and involves quite a ministry. Its importance cannot be overemphasized. It is the calling and the ministry that underlies whatever other calling or vocation belongs to us.

ON THE ROLE OF AMBASSADOR

I remember as a boy how much two words and a song meant to me. They may sound rather naïve and simple but to a poor boy in the west end of Louisville they gave a very special feeling and purpose. Now that I am a senior adult, I realize that there are some things from childhood that need to be recaptured. When I reflect on the truth of the two words and the song, they give me a special feeling and sense of purpose all over again. I believe it is a special feeling and sense of purpose we all ought to have.

The two words are "Royal Ambassadors" based on 2 Corinthians 5:20. It was an organization, similar to the Boy Scouts, that no longer exists. The theme song of the R.A.'s was "The King's Business." It is probably not found in any modern hymnbook. Here is the first verse and chorus as I remember them:

> I am a stranger here, within a foreign land;
> My home is far away, upon a golden strand;
> Ambassador to be of realms beyond the sea,
> I'm here on business for my king.
> This is the message that I bring,
> A message angels fain would sing:
> "O be ye reconciled," Thus saith my Lord & King,
> "O be ye reconciled to God."

The word "ambassador" has other meanings for us, but Paul is projecting his idea against the background of the messengers who went out from Rome to bring a country into the family of the Roman Empire. It was a great privilege to be counted a Roman citizen and to be an official part of the greatest power on earth. The ambassadors brought good news and great opportunity: it was to be a part of the Roman Empire, the most powerful kingdom on earth, with all its privileges and with all its responsibilities. Paul is writing about a greater opportunity: the privilege of bringing the good news of God's invitation for people to become a part of the Kingdom of God, the eternal Kingdom. The way to become a part of that Kingdom is the way of reconciliation.

Ramifications

ASKING THE REALLY BIG QUESTIONS

In the first frame, Snoopy is lying in the door of his doghouse. He is thinking to himself: "Sometimes I lie awake at night wondering why I was born." Frame two: "Why was I put on this earth? What am I doing here?" Frame three: "And then suddenly it hits me…" Frame four: "I haven't the faintest idea."

As with most of Charles Schultz's Peanuts comic strips, they are intended to bring a smile and then to make us think. Even Snoopy is among the philosophers that populate these frames. He asks the inescapable questions that come to all of us: "Why was I put on this earth? What am I doing here?" In Philippians 3:12 Paul writes: *I press on to take hold of that for which Christ Jesus took hold of me.* Really what Paul says is, "I was grabbed for a purpose, now I want to grab that purpose." What he is talking about is his response to the calling that came to him: Philippians 3:14 – "*I press on toward the goal for the prize of the heavenly call of God in Christ Jesus*" (NRSV). Unfortunately, many translations use the word *heavenly* for the Greek word which literally means *upward*. Many associate heavenly with something that is not associated with everyday life in this world. I like to translate upward as high because Paul is convinced he has been grasped for a high calling and he wants to grasp it: "*I press on toward the prize of the high calling of God in Christ Jesus.*

To the age-old question, "Why are you here?", I remember the tongue-in-cheek answer: "Well, everybody's got to be somewhere." Is the life of the believer simply happenstance, luck of the draw, and finally just "a tale told by an idiot, full of sound and fury, signifying nothing"? (Macbeth, Act 5, Scene 5). Calling, purpose, mission – are the things that give us reason to be. They are the things that make it worth getting up in the morning (a decision seniors know is no light matter!). Also, I believe the biblical thesis is that no calling God gives is a small calling. Not one is insignificant. With

God, there are no "lesser" callings. Even if what we do appears to be unnoticed by the world (we need to ask what that would look like and, ultimately, if it really matters!), the fact of an accountability day for everyone means that God certainly takes notice. Taking all these things into account, it is much easier to begin each day with, "*This is the day the Lord has made. I will rejoice and be glad in it*" (Psalm 118:24, NKJV).

RIGHT HERE! RIGHT NOW!

> Thomas Merton: "If I had no choice about the age in which I was to live, I nevertheless have a choice about the attitude I take and about the way and the extent of my participation in its living ongoing events. To choose the world is… an acceptance of a task and a vocation in the world, in history, and in time. In my time, which is the present."[2]

The book of Esther (in which the name of God is never mentioned) contains one of the most quoted verses in Scripture. They are the words Mordecai sends to Esther (his uncle's daughter) when Haman hatches a conspiracy against the Jews: *Who knows whether you have come to the kingdom for such a time as this?*" (Esther 4:14, NKJV). This unlikely Jewish young woman has won a beauty contest and now finds herself queen. Her role as rescuer of her people is not without risk, but she accepts the calling and sends her reply to Mordecai: "*I will go to the king, which is against the law; and if I perish, I perish*" (4:16, NKJV). The Purim festival continues as an annual celebration of the deliverance of the Jews by Esther.

Few of us will receive such a position or such a call. Neither will it come in the dramatic way that Isaiah's call came to him (Isaiah 6:6-13). "Victor Frankl says we detect rather than invent our missions in life. I like that choice of words. I think each of us has an internal monitor or sense…that gives us an awareness of our own uniqueness and the singular contributions that we can

---

2 Jenny Odell, *How to Do Nothing* (Brooklyn: Melville House, 2019), 59.

make."³ Something within us says, "This is what I was made for. This is my purpose. This is what God has put within me; this is why I am here!"

IT OFTEN INVOLVES FINDING THE KAIROS MOMENT IN A CHRONOS WORLD

The Greek language uses two different words for time – *chronos* and *kairos*. *Chronos* is simply time passing, time measured by the ticking of the clock or the pages of a calendar, time as designated in the phrase "time marches on." *Kairos* is a time of opportunity, the right moment, a special moment, a turning point, or as someone has called it, a "light-bulb moment." I call it that moment when time comes alive with meaning, purpose, and insight with history-changing and time-changing dimensions. The Bible is filled with stories of God bringing *kairos* moments into a *chronos* world. In the Greek translation of the Hebrew Scriptures, the word *kairos* appears three times as often as the word *chronos*.

In our day I fear too many feel just as Hamlet did when he cried, "The time is out of joint. O cursed spite, that ever I was born to set it right" (Act 1, Scene 5). The truth is, the time is always out of joint. That is just the nature of *chronos*. What I would say is that no matter how zany or crazy or dark the *chronos* is, God still works in the *kairos* moments. There is an old Sufi story that reveals how God usually does it:

> Past the seeker, as he prayed, came the crippled and the beggar and the beaten. And seeing them, the holy one went down into deep prayer and cried, "Great God, how is it that a loving creator can see such things and yet do nothing about them?" And out of the long silence, God said, "I did do something about them. I made you." (Source unknown).

---

3   Stephen R. Covey, *The 7 Habits of Highly Effective People* (New York: Simon and Schuster, 1989), 128.

CONCLUDING THOUGHTS

The universal calling to be an ambassador of reconciliation is always in the context of our individual life situations and the other callings that structure our vocations, community, and social lives. It is lived out within the unique circumstances that shape our lives. It involves encounters with those in our world. It will ordinarily be done in the ordinary events of our everyday living. It is one of the major demonstrations of what it means to be the salt and light that characterize Jesus' followers (Matthew 5:13-16).

CREATING BRIDGES OF POSSIBILITY

BIBLICAL SOUNDINGS

Luke 19:5 — When Jesus reached the spot, he looked up and said to him, "Zacchaeus, come down, immediately. I must stay at your house today."

HOW TO UPSET THE NEIGHBORHOOD

The crowd's response to Jesus' announcement to Zacchaeus is a study in contrasts: *Descending hastily he (Zacchaeus) welcomed Jesus with joy; but all the onlookers murmured, "He's gone to be the guest of a man well-known to be a sinner"* (19:6-7; SCHONFIELD). In his role as chief tax collector, Zacchaeus was too well-known for his own good. His job meant exclusion from the Synagogue and practically all other normal social contacts as well. The exuberance of the man literally "up a tree and out on a limb" is juxta-positioned with the murmuring of the crowd. Immediately we are reminded of the constant murmuring of the children of Israel as they tromped through the desert wilderness. It was the sound of displeasure and discontent; it was their commentary on things that ought not to be as they were. So it was with the shocking news that Jesus was going to spend the day in the home of a notorious collaborator with Rome.

Tax collectors "were regarded as quislings, and renegades and traitors....Robbers, murderers, and tax collectors were classed together."[1] No one has ever given the reasons so clearly as William Barclay:

> The Roman custom was to farm out the taxes. They assessed a district at a certain figure, and then they sold the right to collect the taxes to the highest bidder. So long as the buyer handed over the assessed figure at the end of the year, he was entitled to retain whatever else he could extract from the people.[2]
>
> The stated taxes were bad enough: a poll tax for all men from 14 to 64 and all women 12 to 65; a ground tax of ten percent of all grain grown and 20 percent of wine and oil; and an income tax of one percent of income. Then there were all kinds of duties: a tax for using the roads, the harbors, and the markets; a tax on a cart, each wheel, and on the animal that drew it; and all kinds of import and export duties.[3]

Zacchaeus was an outcast because this is where he belonged – cast out. But on this fateful day, Jesus threw out a bridge of possibility. The possibility of including the excluded has always upset the neighborhood.

It's The Attempt To Make The First Connection

John 3:16 – *God so loved the world that he gave his one and only Son...*

Luke 19:10 – *The Son of Man came to seek and to save what was lost.*

Matthew 9:11 – *When the Pharisees saw this, they asked his disciples, "Why does your teacher eat with tax collectors and sinners?"*

When God sent his son into the world, we don't see anywhere the instruction, "Don't waste your time on the hopeless." As far as

---

[1] William Barclay, *The Gospel of Luke* (Philadelphia: The Westminster Press, 1956), 61.
[2] Ibid.
[3] Ibid.

the biblical witness is concerned, no one was written off, no one was off-limits, no one was beyond the reach of God's love, no one was outside the circle of grace. This is the basic assumption of Scripture and the clear agenda in Jesus' ministry. There was no "lostness" that was beyond the possibility of "being found." Jesus never met a hopeless case. He never said, "I don't have time to waste on this unredeemable situation."

God's grace, mercy, and love have always been seeking those whose lostness takes many forms and has many dimensions: lost from purpose, lost in self-centeredness, lost from meaningful relationships, lost in anger and fear, lost in addiction, lost in despair and hopelessness, lost in missing God's mark for life, lost in falling short of the glory that God has placed within each human life. There is no lostness that is not on the list of God's seeking and his ability to save. Jesus took over the agenda of the Father's reconciling purposes when he came to pitch his tent among us (John 1:14). Some Pharisees could not understand why Jesus was eating with tax collectors and sinners (those who rejected strict Temple religion). Not only was it detrimental to his reputation but surely his time could have been better used with those who were champions of God's righteous causes in the world.

My favorite translations of Psalm 23:6 are: *Only goodness and faithful love **will pursue** me all the days of my life* (HOLMAN); *Kindness and faithful love **pursue me** every day of my life* (NJB). The traditional *will follow me* is not necessarily incorrect, it simply does not carry the impact of God's intentionality. God's goodness and faithful love are not trailing along behind us; they are attempting to overtake us. It is reconciliation and relationship that God desires with his creation as clearly demonstrated in the Garden of Eden story. Even then, when things go wrong, God comes seeking and finding and building bridges.

Ours Is The Input, Not The Outcome

1 Corinthians 3:6-7 – *I planted the seed, Apollos watered it, but God has been making it grow. So neither the one who plants nor the one who waters is anything, but only God who makes things grow.*

Once you lift the burden of results from your life, you are free to explore and attempt things you would never have done before. Once the only requirement becomes to do what you believe you ought to do to the best of your ability and leave the results with God, life takes wing. To a church with divided loyalties, Paul places his efforts next to others who are simply sowing the seeds of the gospel; the harvest depends on God's miracle of growth. The only failure on Paul's part would be to refuse to do the work of input; God will take care of outcome.

Not every bridge we attempt to build will be completed; many we build will not be crossed by those on the other side. Reconciliation on God's part has always been an offer. Do we have to say it? God is not like the "godfather": he never makes us an offer we can't refuse. The right to refuse is written into every promise God makes. Moses echoes this in Deuteronomy 30:19 – *This day I call the heavens and the earth as witnesses against you that I have set before you life and death, blessings and curses. Now choose life, so that you and your children may live.* Even Moses could not build a bridge of reconciliation the Israelites were compelled to cross.

It cannot be repeated often enough: God is not the one who needs to be reconciled. All that is necessary for his reconciling stance has been fulfilled in the gift of his Son. Christ's death and resurrection have reconstructed the bridge that our sin and rejection destroyed. Although there is no specific doctrine of "atonement" in Scripture, everything points to the decisive cross and resurrection event as God's way of dealing with sin, death, and evil. Jesus' paying the price for sin, the offering of himself as the supreme sacrifice, the taking of our place on the cross – these are all attempts to articulate what was involved in the great mystery of God's redemption through his Son.

Even Paul could only say, "*We implore you, be reconciled with God*" (2 Corinthians 5:20). He made the offer. He attempted to build bridges that could be crossed. He attempted to open the way, to make reconciliation possible. The word possibility is our word today. With so many blowing up bridges (literally and figuratively), we are engaged in the ministry of possibility. We can't make it happen but we can make it possible. In this world, that is a big assignment. But it is ours.

Ramifications

Let's Ditch The Heavy-Handed Approaches

From my files, I found this story which appeared in an Atlanta newspaper almost three decades ago. It is the story of a young mother who was unsuccessfully attempting to give some liquid medicine to her two-year-old son. Nothing she did could persuade him to take the medicine. Finally, in frustration and despair, she threw down the spoon and fled in tears to her bedroom. In a few minutes, she heard loud laughter coming from the kitchen. She went to investigate and found that the grandmother had solved the problem. She had mixed the medicine with orange juice, put it in a water pistol, and was shooting it into the wide-open mouth of the delighted youngster. My interpretation: the grandmother built a bridge with a difficult two-year-old. Everything was changed from tears to laughter because a bridge of possibility had been built.

I doubt that anyone, child or adult, was ever persuaded to do something they didn't want to do with the words, "You will do this because it is right and because it is good for you!" These are not persuasive or bridge-building words. We continue to be in the midst of the COVID pandemic which should by now be under control. Many in the medical community are convinced it is those who are refusing to be vaccinated who are causing the extension. The media is awash in misinformation, cries of socialized medicine, and demands that personal freedom must come first. Heavy-handed approaches have not worked with the hold-outs who sincerely believe they have legitimate reasons for their reluctance to take the shots. As the grandmother met the two-year-old where he was, I believe we must always meet people where they are if we are to have any chance at bridge-building. How do you believe the creative grandmother might deal with this situation?

THINK AGAIN!

The above heading is the title of a thought-provoking book by Adam Grant. In the chapter, "Dances With Foes: How to Win Debates and Influence People," he gives three strategies that I am applying to bridge-building:[4]

1. The more anger and hostility the other person expresses, the more curiosity and interest you show.
2. In a heated argument, you can always stop and ask, "What evidence would change your mind." If the answer is "nothing," then there's no point in continuing the debate.
3. By asking questions rather than thinking for the audience, we invite them to join us as a partner and think for themselves.

The reason I like the above suggestions is that they make me responsible for creating new possibilities in the conversation. These sentences got two stars when I read them:

> Compassion is the act of opening your heart. To live in a state of compassion means you approach the world with your emotional barriers lowered and your ability to connect with others intact.
>
> The key to learning the lesson of compassion is realizing that you are in control of the construction or destruction of those barriers that create distance between you and others.[5]

---

4 Adam Grant, *Think Again* (New York: Viking, 2021), 115, 116, 119.
5 Cherie Carter-Scott, *If Life is a Game… These Are the Rules* (Naperville, IL: Simple Truths, 1998), 45, 51.

The best illustration of this principle I know is the story one of my students told in a seminary class I was teaching. It occurred the previous summer while she was working as a waitress. Two or three times a week a woman came in who always ordered a diet plate and iced Sanka. If things were not exactly right, she sent back the order. She was especially upset if too much of the ice had melted in her coffee. The student said she learned the secret of serving the coffee: she brought a glass of ice to the table and poured the Sanka over it. Still, the woman sat before her with pursed lips, in spite of the fact that the waitress was always kind and gracious to her. One day the woman came in and said, "Well, you won't have to put up with me any longer." The student asked, "Why?" "I'm leaving for two weeks and when I get back you will be gone to school." The student said she had an overwhelming urge and she acted on it. She reached out and hugged the woman – who wouldn't let her go! When she finally did, she asked the waitress to sit down with her. She poured out her heart about the death of her husband, her constant loneliness, and the many negative things that had filled her life. She invited the student over to her house for a meal. When the student married later that summer, the woman gave her several servings of her silverware pattern. They still keep in contact.

WHAT THIS STUDENT DID IS WHAT WE ALL ARE CALLED TO DO

> Anyone who offers you an easy path is to be mistrusted. Life is difficult and messy; there is no point trying to mask that or pretend otherwise. But every situation you encounter is in need of one thing: a holy moment....Allow God to raise up the saint in you. This is what your corner of the world needs right now.[6]

Matthew Kelly, from whom the above quote comes, continues to be one of my favorite writers. His inspiration, practicality, and

---

6   Matthew Kelly, *Rediscover the Saints* (North Palm Beach: Blue Sparrow, 2019), 12.

challenges seem tailor-made for the kind of world in which we now find ourselves. The student who told the class her story I related above, created a holy moment by allowing God to raise up the saint in her. When Paul addresses the church at Corinth, he calls them "saints," not as some potential, but as who they are. The NKJV translates 1 Corinthians 1:2 in a misleading way: *To the church of God which is at Corinth, to those who are sanctified in Christ Jesus, called TO BE saints...* The words to be are in italics which, means they are not a part of the Greek text. Omitting these added words, Paul addresses those in the church at Corinth as *those called saints*!

I have often heard someone say, "Well, I'm certainly no saint!" I immediately want to reply, "Oh, yes you are!" The problem is that the word "saint" has too often been associated with perfection and those who have received a special designation. Biblically, all believers are saints – God's designated ones, God's holy ones – who have said "Yes" to the reconciling invitation of God.

I have often wanted to say to someone, "Don't you realize who you are?" I think more of us should adopt the philosophy that Wayne Oates adopted and lived out in his truly saintly life.

> My calling since that time at Mars Hill College has been gently to take off the cheap price tags people place on themselves and ask their permission to bestow the price tag God our heavenly Parent has placed on us with a love that is more than human love. For this nobody need walk in shame for any reason.[7]

Of his fifty-three books, his biography from which this quote is taken, *The Struggle to be Free*, remains my favorite. I hear his voice in the printed words and I vividly remember so many of the holy moments he created for me and my congregation. He allowed God to raise up the saint in him for much more than a small corner of his world. In his life and ministry, I cannot begin to imagine how many seemingly impossible bridges for which he was responsible.

---

7   Wayne Oates, *The Struggle to be Free* (Philadelphia: Westminster Press, 1983), 43-44.

Concluding Thoughts

Creating bridges of possibility basically results from the kind of persons we are and the simple actions that invite, rather than erect barriers. We take the initiative in reaching out to others as God takes the initiative in reaching out to each of us. We don't wait for the phone to ring, for the email to appear, or for the post office to deliver the letter. Bridges of possibility mean that we are in the ones who make the call, send the email, or write the letter. Our basic assumption is that we are always called on to make the first move.

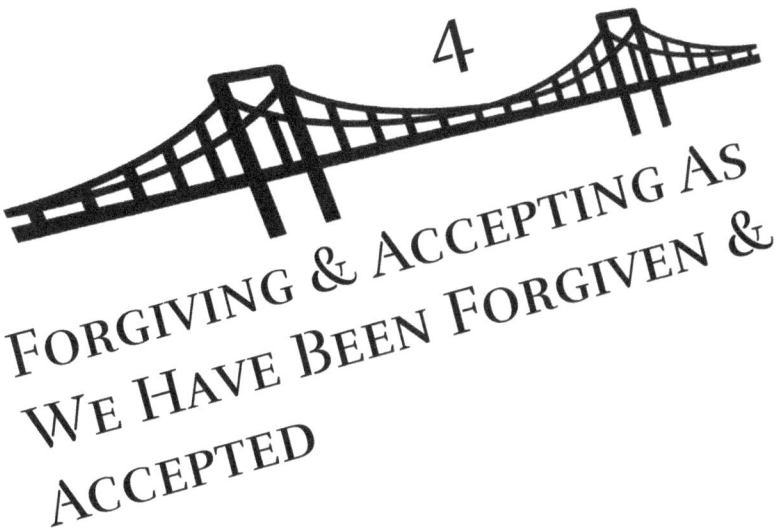

Forgiving & Accepting as We Have Been Forgiven & Accepted

Biblical Soundings

Matthew 18:32-33 — Then the master called the servant in. "You wicked servant," he said, "I cancelled all that debt of yours because you begged me to. Shouldn't you have had mercy on your fellow servant just as I had on you?"

Context! Context! Context!

The parable of the unforgiving servant follows Peter's question of how often he should forgive someone who sins against him (18:21). (Peter begins with the assumption that he is the one who will be wronged. It does not occur to him to ask how often someone he sins against should forgive him.) To Peter's seemingly generous "seven times" (the rabbis suggested three times), Jesus dispenses with counting and declares that seventy-seventy times (or seventy times seven) is the correct "calculation." Meaning: you can't apply mathematics to forgiveness; you must learn to be a forgiving person.

Immediately, Jesus introduces his parable with strong and connecting words that can be variously translated: *For this reason the kingdom of heaven may to compared to...*(NRSV); *Thus the Kingdom of Heaven has been likened to...*(LATTIMORE); *That is why the Kingdom of Heaven can be likened to...*(BARCLAY); *For this reason, the kingdom of heaven can be compared to...*(HOLMAN); *Thus the Kingdom of the heavens has been likened to....*(HART).

We are talking about Kingdom issues and the radical place that forgiveness plays in the lives of the Followers of the Way. This is not an incidental aside to being a disciple; it is one of the cardinal principles. Jesus uses outrageous numbers in his requirements for forgiving others and draws unbelievable disparity in the difference between the debts of two of a king's servants. That is why people could never forget his teachings or his parables. They marked a new day, a new time, the truly good and the "gospel" (good news) as no one had ever before heard it.

Getting The Correct Perspective

Jesus' story (Matthew 18:32-33) is about accounting day for two of a king's servants. The first owed the king ten thousand talents. The TNIV translates it as *ten thousand bags of gold* with a footnote indicating that a talent was worth about 20 years of a day laborer's wages (18:24). Barclay gives the English twist and tells us that the servant owes 2,400,000 pounds (remember: that was written in the 1950s). When the king threatens to sell him and his family into slavery to repay the debt, the servant begs for mercy. The king cancels the debt and lets him go.

The unbelievable amount of the debt owned and the unbelievable generosity of the king stand side by side. We are not told how such a debt was accumulated, only that the due date had arrived (another sermon leaps from the text at this point!). The inability of the servant to repay is abundantly clear. Mercy and forgiveness are the only solutions. Working out a payment plan is never in the cards - not with these kinds of numbers. The enormity of the debt and the immeasurable forgiveness dispensed are beyond comprehension. That is the point of the parable. Jesus' unstated question to Peter is, "Do you see yourself in this parable?" That is his question to each of us.

IT'S THE OLD LOG AND SPECK PROBLEM ALL OVER AGAIN

When Jesus asks how we are able to see the speck in our neighbor's eye and not be aware of the log in our own eye (Matthew 7:3), he's talking about a universal problem. (More about this in chapter 7.) The faults of others always loom larger than our own; speck detection is so much easier than log awareness. I suspect that most of these logs have to do with *the weightier matters of the law* that Jesus accused some of the scribes and Pharisees of ignoring: *justice, mercy, and faith* (Matthew 23:23, NRSV). Jesus takes the speck and log comparison a step further when he charges the scribes and Pharisees with the absurdity: *You strain out a gnat and swallow a camel!* (23:24).

Grace, mercy, forgiveness, justice, and love are the weightier matters of the law. They form the foundation on which our ethical and social principles stand. They come first. In 1 Corinthians 13, Paul boldly states that if we do not first have love, nothing else we do really matters. I believe we can almost say the same thing about all the weightier matters of the law. For me, Jesus' words and deeds make the case for such a position.

The kicker in the parable comes when the forgiven servant meets a fellow servant who owes him some money – a hundred denarii (which was the wage of a day laborer: Matthew 20:2). The TNIV puts the debt at a hundred silver coins in contrast to the ten thousand bags of gold owed by the first servant. Barclay puts the second servant's debt at 5 pounds in comparison to the 2,400,000 pounds owed by the first servant. One is quite a log and the other, by comparison, is hardly even a speck. When we contemplate God's grace, mercy, and forgiveness in our own lives, can we not see its magnitude? How can we possibly withhold mercy and forgiveness when God's generosity has been so overwhelming in our own lives? That is the question posed by the parable. It's not my question; it's the question Jesus asks each of us.

THE VERB TENSE IS A GRABBER

When we pray The Disciple's Prayer (commonly called The Lord's Prayer), a correct verb tense often goes unnoticed. The KJV, where most of us began, reads: *Forgive us our debts, as we forgive our debtors* (Matthew 6:12). The more accurate reading is: *Forgive us our debts, as we also HAVE FORGIVEN our debtors* (TNIV). We stand ready to receive God's forgiveness because forgiveness has already been moving in our lives toward our brothers and sisters. We are already known as forgiving persons. (The subject of forgiveness would require another book to fully explore its dimensions and ramifications.)

Jesus' gives this brief commentary on his model prayer in Matthew 6:14-15 – *For if you forgive others when they sin against you, your heavenly Father will also forgive you. But if you do not forgive others their sins, your Father will not forgive your sins.* My interpretation of this text is that if we refuse to forgive others, we have closed the door through which God's forgiveness flows to us. An unforgiving spirit blocks God's forgiving Spirit. An unforgiving spirit establishes a roadblock, a barrier, a wall. It seems to me that it is not that God does not desire to forgive us but that he is unable to do so because of the stop sign we have erected.

WE ARE REALLY TALKING ABOUT GOD'S ACCEPTANCE OF US AS WE ARE

Sacrifices have always been part of almost every religious tradition. Many had to do with atonement for wrongdoing. The gods would receive the offering and remove the separation. There would be an AT-ONE-MENT and relationship would be restored. In the Christian tradition, God himself provided the final and ultimate sacrifice that once and for all time established redemption and reconciliation. God's offer of grace, forgiveness, and acceptance only depend on our "Yes" to his offer.

As always, God made the first move: *But God demonstrates his own love for us in this: while we were still sinners, Christ died for us* (Romans 5:8). We didn't have to "get right" with God before he would "get right" with us. We have been loved and accepted, faults, fractures, sins and all. God's acceptance of us has been total and unconditional. We can receive his grace and forgiveness just as we are without getting our house in order before we do so. The getting of our house in order comes afterward and is the work of a lifetime.

I am convinced that far too many don't really believe (or feel) that God's love and acceptance of them is total and unconditional. As a consequence, they have difficulty loving and accepting others – with all their shortcomings. I don't think you can give acceptance you have not experienced. I don't think you can give love you have not experienced. To feel loved and accepted just as we are is God's greatest gift to us; it is the only preparation for a life of love and acceptance.

Ramifications

Rejection By Category

> "Dr. Grant and Dr. Sattler," Hammond said. "It's good of you to join me. Allow me to introduce my associate, Donald Gennaro." Gennaro was a stocky, muscular man in his mid-thirties wearing an Armani suit and wire-frame glasses. Grant disliked him on sight. He shook hands quickly. When Ellie shook hands, Gennaro said in surprise, "You're a woman." "These things happen," she said, and Grant thought: "She doesn't like him either."[1]

In the book which became the basis for the movie blockbuster *Jurassic Park*, comes this early dialogue expressing surprise that a

---

1   Michael Crichton, *Jurassic Park* (New York: Alfred A. Knopf, 1990), 64.

paleontologist could be a woman. Put any other person of either sex or of any other race or culture and ask if you can picture them in any profession or position. More and more in our current culture, the question would be, "Why not?" Why would a door be closed because of who a person is by birth? Gennaro's amazement reflects the question Nathaniel asks Phillip: "*Can anything good come out of Nazareth?*" (John 1:24). Judging by categories saves so much time; you don't have to bother with getting to know the individual person. There must have been something about Gennaro's demeanor (aside from his appearance) that tipped off his prior judgments as to who was in and who was out in the scientific field.

A basis for judgment that is non-biblical and parallels the above example is much more frequent in our culture:

> Neville Alexander once said, "Once the commodity value of people displaces their intrinsic human worth or dignity we are well on the way to a state of barbarism."…The severely unequal distribution, the fact that the most difficult labor on Earth, for example, cutting sugar cane, is paid only $2-$3 a day, while others get millions a day, (should) be seen as criminal."[2]

To value a person on the basis of their contribution to the local (or world) economy, will not be found in Scripture. In the parable that opens this section, it is obvious that the first servant holds a very high position in the King's administration. His debt reflects the lifestyle of a wealthy man who probably let his enthusiasm for high living distort his financial capabilities. His prestige and apparent wealth kept him in the best circles with all the right people. The second servant in the story has no such position. His debt probably reflects a few coins tossed one day to provide food for a family always living on the edge. His job for the King was one that almost anyone could fill and was definitely minimum wage. (It may have involved sweeping out the stables.) He was certainly not listed in Who's Who in the Kingdom.

---

2 Steven Klees, *The Conscience of a Progressive* (Winchester, UK: Zero Books, 2020), 85.

The king's canceling of the first servant's enormous debt should have resulted in compassion for the "lesser servant's" debt. Perhaps the first servant saw himself as deserving of forgiveness and worth more to the king and society in general. The king's fury at learning of his lack of compassion resulted in harsh judgment. The parable is rich in possible interpretations but some things seem clear. There are no "lesser servants" and all of our fellow servants (what all of us are in this world) deserve the same kind of acceptance, compassion, and forgiveness that we have received. They are of equal worth regardless of where they stand on the culture's ladder of success. After all, that is the culture's ladder; it is not God's ladder.

Jesus Never Met An "Other"

> "We know what it's like to be different, don't we?" Ron asked. "I thought about it the first time I saw you when you came off that river. When I saw you I thought to myself, 'He's an other,' just like me. You and me, we know what it's like to look out at the world from a dark place. And when people see us coming they see something damaged. They see something inferior to them. Right, Kyle?"[3]

From the pages of a modern novel, comes the reflection of what it feels like to be seen as "damaged goods," as an "other." When Jesus' disciples were asked why their Teacher was eating with tax collectors and sinners (Matthew 9:9-13), it was assumed that no religious teacher would be associating with these "others." Tax collectors were "ritually" unclean; they were outcasts, they were damaged goods. "Many people in America today think they are followers of Christ, or that they 'know' the Bible, but have they read it? If they have, wouldn't they know that Jesus preached a message of "radical inclusiveness" or "radical welcoming?"[4] I would add to this: Jesus lived a message of radical acceptance.

---

3   C. J. Box, *Paradise Valley* (New York: Minotaur Books, 2018), 281.
4   Jimmy R. Watson, *Jesus is Still Speaking Through the Gospel of Mark* (Bloomington: Xlibris, 2011), 95.

A necessary Sidebar: "…we are all damaged goods. Some persons are so damaged that they are incapable of genuine dialogue. They cannot allow any other to be genuinely other."[5] This is one of the major reasons that, sometimes, bridges of possibility are impossible. There will always be extremists who insist on "my way or the highway." Persistence, patience, and a miracle might one day make an extended hand acceptable, but I have found it very difficult to reconcile with those who will tolerate no "other."

The theme song of a popular T.V. show of many years ago, asks the question that almost everyone would answer "Yes!": "Wouldn't you like to go to a place where everybody knows your name…a place where everybody's glad you came?" This was the theme song of *Cheers*, a sitcom about a bar. It ought to be the theme song of every church. It was certainly the theme song of the banquet the tax collector Matthew gave at his home where Jesus was the host and the others found a place.

There is a famous remark attributed to the late Zsa Zsa Gabor which probably (if true) was tongue-in-cheek: "I went to this gigantic party, darling, but it was so dull. I was the only one there I'd ever heard of." The message of the gospel is that every individual is a VIP in the sight of God and he has heard of every one of us! He knows us all by name.

When Jesus found people who believed they were numbered among the others and felt they were damaged goods, he never left them that way. It was my privilege to hear the late William Augustus Jones at a Stetson Pastor's School. He used one of the most fascinating sermon titles I have ever heard. He called his sermon, "Jesus, the Junk Man." Among the things he said (from my notes): "The God I serve doesn't throw anybody away. God is in the restoration and reclamation business. Jesus is a junk man. He goes around and picks up scraps of humanity and puts them together for something glorious."

---

5   David Tracy, *Fragments* (Chicago: The University of Chicago Press, 2020), 156.

The bridge between Jesus' answer to Peter's question of how many times he should forgive someone who sins against him, is: *Therefore, the kingdom of heaven is like a king who wanted to settle accounts with his servants* (Matthew 18:23). We are challenged to be forgiving and accepting of others without weighing their damaged condition, their "other" status, or seeing anything in them that makes them "lesser" as a human being than we are. We have experienced such an abundance of God's grace, mercy, compassion, and the never-ending stream of his forgiveness and acceptance, it only seems a given that we will extend the same to those who need it from us.

One of my all-time heroes is Tom Landry. Much has been written about him, including Bob St. John's *Landry: the Legend and the Legacy*.[6] On the endorsement page of the book, Billy Graham is quoted: "Tom was one of the greatest Christian gentlemen I ever knew." My favorite story comes from many years ago when the Ohio State coach, Woody Hayes, was fired for hitting an opposing player during a football game. He confessed that he had lost control during the game and did something uncalled for. He lost his job, his reputation, and his friends. At the end of the season, a banquet was held for professional athletes. At that banquet, seated with Tom Landry as his guest, was Woody Hayes.

Concluding Thoughts

Forgiveness and acceptance are basic to all human relationships. Both of these call for humility, patience, and courage as we explore what we ourselves have needed and see all "others" in that same need.

Forgiveness and acceptance are open doors to conversation and walking together. Judgment (an unforgiving spirit) and prejudice are closed doors, locked from the inside.

---

6   Bob St. John, *Landry: the Legend and the Legacy* (Nashville: Word Publishing, 2000), endorsement page.

5

Refusing to Make Our Ways and Standards Universal

Biblical Soundings

Mark 9:38-40 — *"Teacher," said John, "we saw someone driving out demons in your name and we told him to stop because he was not one of us." "Do not stop him," Jesus said. "No one who does a miracle in my name can in the next moment say anything bad about me, for whoever is not against us is for us."*

Here is a problem that never seems to go away: an unnamed "someone" is performing exorcisms in Jesus' name but he is not with the group of twelve. He is not an "us," he is a "them." When you read the Gospel as a whole, the irony of the situation is inescapable. Shortly before this episode, while Peter, James, and John are witnessing the Transfiguration (Mark 9:14-18), at the foot of the mountain, the remainder of the disciples are involved in an argument with a distressed father. Coming down from the mountain, Jesus encounters a large crowd and asks what the argument is all about. *A man in the crowd answered, "Teacher I brought you my son, who is possessed by a spirit....I asked your disciples to drive out the spirit, but they could not."*

An old story I heard so many years ago that I can't remember when is really the perennial story. In the days of early America, on a Sunday morning, two ministers on horseback were making their way to their respective small rural churches. Friends for years, they had made this ride many times. In the course of their conversation, one said, "I think it is commendable that, although we are of different denominations, you and I have been close friends for so many years, each of serving the Lord in our different communities of faith." "Yes," replied the other, "that is true. Each of us is doing the Lord's work – you in your way, and I in His."

If there is a corrective anywhere in the New Testament to John's attitude, it is Paul's stance in his letter to the Philippians: *It is true that some preach Christ out of envy and rivalry, but others out of goodwill. The latter do so out of love, knowing that I am put here for the defense of the gospel. The former preach Christ out of selfish ambition, not sincerely, supposing that they can stir up trouble for me while I am in chains. But what does it matter? The important thing is that in every way, whether from false motives or true, Christ is preached. And because of this I rejoice* (Philippians 1:15-18).

The parallel is clear: the healer who was being challenged by John was being used to heal people. Those who were opposed to Paul and his methods were nonetheless preaching Christ. Mission accomplished, even by those who were not in the same "us" group. And so has it ever been. So why not rejoice?

John 10:16 – "*I have other sheep that are not of this sheep pen. I much bring them also. They too will listen to my voice, and there shall be one flock and one shepherd.*"

Verb tenses can make a big difference in the interpretation of a text. The Wuest translation provides not so much a correction as it does a clarification: *And other sheep I have which are not of this sheepfold. Those also it is necessary in the nature of the case for me to lead, and my voice they shall listen to, and there shall come to be one flock, one shepherd.* The Montgomery translation provides the same clarification: *I have other sheep also, which do not belong to this fold.*

I must bring them too, and they will listen to my voice, and they will become one flock, one shepherd.

There shall come to be and they will become places the emphasis on a future unity, not a present one. The diversity among Christians has always been disturbing to many and critics attempt to use the divisions as evidence of a flawed faith. It appears that Jesus' disciples (in Matthew 9) couldn't imagine another unaffiliated group doing the Lord's work. For all kinds of reasons, there have always been differences of opinion and emphases among believers. Much of this developed after the Scriptures became available to the general public and an "official interpretation" of texts no longer was acceptable. Instead of seeing this as negative, it may be viewed as the affirmation of what Catherine Marshall is once credited as saying: "God finds the secret stairway into every human heart." Even in matters of faith, one size does not seem to fit all.

The longed-for unity, according to John 10:16, comes with the devotion to the shepherd and the willingness to listen to his voice and follow his leading. I think it is no small matter that the first confession of faith appears to have been "Jesus is Lord." Paul writes in his most developed theological treatise: "*If you declare with your mouth 'Jesus is Lord,' and believe in your heart that God raised him from the dead, you will be saved*" (Romans 10:9). The center of our faith is a person whom we believe to be the Anointed One, the Messiah. Our unity is based on our oneness in him.

The possibilities of who those other sheep are, are limitless according to what Jesus says in Luke 13:29 – *People will come from east and west and north and south, and will take their places in the feast in the kingdom of God.* Most of us are guilty of narrowing the ways in which God works and limiting the kinds of people with whom he works. The Scriptures are full of references where Jesus "colors outside the lines" of the usually acceptable candidates for the Kingdom. In chapters eight and nine we will speak further of how the unlimited dimensions of God's love and grace contribute to surprises and possibilities that continue to astonish us.

Ramifications

As It Was In The Beginning, Is Now, And Forever Shall Be

> There is no innocent tradition; there is no innocent text; there is no innocent reading, including this one. All our religious traditions are pluralistic, complex, fragmentary, and ambiguous in their histories and effects in cultures and societies.[1]

The world in which Jesus lived was marked by complex and diverse interpretations of the Jewish tradition. There was no singular "Jewish faith." The Sadducees and Pharisees not only disagreed with Jesus on certain issues, they disagreed with one another on such basics as the belief in an afterlife (the Pharisees affirmative and the Sadducees negative). A cursive reading of early church history shows the same kind of diversity among the churches. The above quote from David Tracy is a healthy reminder of what is perfectly normal in religious traditions: "pluralistic, complex, fragmentary, and ambiguous."

A parable in the form of a first-person story:[2]

> I was walking across a bridge one day, and I saw a man standing on the edge, about to jump off. So I ran over and said, "Stop! Don't do it!"
> "Why shouldn't I?" he said.
> "Well, there's so much to live for."
> "Like what?"
> "Well, are you religious?"
> He said yes.
> I said, "Me, too! Are you Christian or Buddhist?"
> "Christian."
> "Me, too! Are you Catholic or Protestant?"
> "Protestant,"

---

1 David Tracy, *Fragments*, 159.
2 Emo Philips, *GQ*, (June 1999), 251.

"Me, too! Are you Episcopalian or Baptist?"

"Baptist."

"Wow, me, too! Are you Baptist Church of God or Baptist Church of the Lord?"

"Baptist Church of God!"

"Me, too! Are you original Baptist Church of God, or are you Reformed Baptist Church of God?"

"Reformed Baptist Church of God!"

"Me, too! Are you Reformed Baptist Church of God, reformation of 1879, or Reformed Baptist Church of God, reformation of 1915?"

He said, "Reformed Baptist Church of God, reformation 1915!"

I shouted, "Heretic!" and pushed him off the bridge.

I find it interesting that this conversation/parable takes place on a bridge. We probably have all been witness to more pushing off the bridge than we have to walking with a brother or sister to the other end of the bridge. Such is the nature of radical convictions and the refusal to recognize those who are not in our sheepfold.

The Ugliest Word In The English Language

Carl Sandburg was once asked, "What is the ugliest word in the English language?" His reply: "Exclusive." Exclusive makes me and mine feel special, superior, privileged, favored, and entitled – which means it separates, creates distance, builds walls, generates suspicion, and fosters animosity and hatred. It's bad enough when the word exclusive is associated with civic and social life, but it is particularly devastating when it is rooted in the Christian faith. Jesus refused to let his disciples coin it for themselves and I am certain that he won't grant us permission to do it.

I remember during my seminary days, taking a break after lunch to watch the "Houseparty" TV show. I tuned in to watch the segment where Art Linkletter talked with children. Art's conversation with the young son of a minister was especially enlightening.

(The L indicates Linkletter and P.K. stands for "preacher's kid," the unfortunate tag of, hopefully, a by-gone era – although both my sons received it on more than one occasion):

> L. "What do you want to be when you grow up?
> P.K. "A preacher like my father."
> L. "What does he do most of the time?"
> P.K. "He talks Christians into becoming Methodists."
> L. "Do you think he could get me into heaven? After all, I'm a Baptist."
> P.K. "He'd just put you on a Methodist jet plane and shoot you up there."
> L. "Where is heaven?"
> P.K. "Oh, it's about twenty miles past Mars."
> L. "What do you think it looks like?"
> P.K. "Everyone's lying around on pink clouds eating angel food."
> L. "Baptists, too?"
> P.K. "They get smaller pieces."

Although this young man was the star of that particular episode, I'm certain he did not maintain that status in a subsequent discussion with his father, whom I'm sure could hardly stop laughing. Perhaps this piece of humor is a better way to show just how absurd an exclusive attitude can be.

GREAT MINDS DON'T THINK ALIKE

The above line is the title of a book by Emily Gosling that carries the subtitle: *"Discover the method & madness of 56 creative geniuses."*[3] The book delivers what it promises and I discovered that, even in similar fields, the techniques and methods are totally different. "One size doesn't fit all" applies to all of the great minds discussed in this brief volume. Three writers illustrate the diversity: Nick Cave says that the artistic process is "just hard labor." His formula: "I wake. I write. I eat. I write. I watch TV." Most importantly, he says you must be sure to constantly flex the mind's imaginative

---
3 Emily Gosling, *Great Minds Don't Think Alike* (London: ILEX, 2018).

powers. "You can write really anywhere if your imagination is in good shape. It needs to be exercised."[4] Agatha Christie claimed usually to have half a dozen notebooks on hand, and these were filled with everything....She was always working on at least two novels at any one time.[5] Gertrude Stein revealed that she was only ever able to write for about 30 minutes each day.[6]

Most people are not going to be open to a relationship that insists on conformity to one method, one schedule, one technique, or one anything. The church of which I was a member when I was young, had as its slogan: "The right to fellowship across honest differences of opinion." I would enlarge that by adding: "different ways of viewing things, different ways of doing things, different ways of dealing with things." In the text from Mark 9:38-40, I'm certain the disciples knew they were in the right group and doing things the right way because Jesus was with them and not anyone else. They felt certain they had a corner on the "Jesus market." But did they? Evidently, some others had heard Jesus' teaching and had responded to his message, and had begun to minister in his name. Undoubtedly, their ministry had a different tone and texture, but Jesus' rebuke to the judgmental disciples appears to indicate that it was, indeed, his ministry as well.

A Little Bit Of History

> Linus looks on as Peppermint Patty begins writing a paper for school. At the top in bold letters she writes : CHURCH HISTORY. She pauses, looks ahead, and puts the pencil to her lips in a moment of contemplation. She then begins: "When writing about church history, we have to go back to the very beginning. Our pastor was born in 1930....

A reading of church history is indeed a revelation for those who want to "get back to the New Testament church." That is a

---

4   Ibid, 17.
5   Ibid, 31
6   Ibid, 69.

phrase I heard many times growing up in a church that was convinced it was one of those churches. Strictly speaking, there was no single New Testament church. There were scattered assemblies (the word used that we translate church) throughout the Roman empire. The diversity of those assemblies is evident from the New Testament letters we have addressed to them. A tongue-in-cheek quip from my file of quotations, reveals our present diversity: "There are more than 22,000 denominations in the world. How lucky you are that you happen to be in the one that is right!" (Juan Carlos Ortiz).

The efforts to enforce uniformity of belief and worship reveals the tragic side of church history. When there was no separation between church and state, it was a given that the church would use the power of the state to eliminate deviant practices. *Wide as the Waters* is an excellent book by Benson Bobrick on the story of the English Bible and the unbelievable carnage left in the wake of efforts to make certain everyone heard only the one true translation of the Bible.[7] Here is the first paragraph in the Prologue of the book:

> The first question ever asked by an Inquisitor of a "heretic" was whether he knew any part of the Bible in his own tongue. It was asked in 1233 of a man who belonged to a dissident religious sect known as the Waldensians, which emphasized Bible study and lay preaching; and it would be asked again of thousands of others before the course of history would render its dark implications null and void.[8]

The powers that ruled church and state felt that to maintain uniformity and orthodoxy it was necessary to keep the Bible in the hands of those who were "qualified" to read and interpret it. They were correct. When average people got their hands on the words of Scripture, all diversity broke loose! I maintain that is the best thing that ever happened because it gave people the right to find and live out their faith as they understood the Scriptures to be speaking to them in their time and place.

---

7 Benson Bobrick, *Wide as the Waters* (New York: Simon and Schuster, 2001).
8 Ibid, 11.

"Eldad and Medad are Prophesying In The Camp."

That is what a young man runs up and tells Moses (Numbers 11:27).

> And Joshua, son of Nun, the assistant of Moses, one of his chosen men, said, "My lord Moses, stop them!" But Moses said to him, "Are you jealous for my sake? Would that all the Lord's people were prophets, and that the Lord would put his spirit on them!" (Numbers 11:28-29).

Many years ago, on a Saturday afternoon in Richmond, Virginia, we got a phone call. Pat answered the call and I heard her hesitantly say, "Yes." There was a pause and another hesitant, "Yes." After a few moments, she began an animated conversation with the person on the line. When she completed the call, I asked, "Who was that?"

Pat replied, "Well, when I answered the phone, the person on the other end asked, 'Sister Pat?' I answered, 'Yes.' Then she said, 'This is Sister Ann. Hobart and Sandy (friends from seminary days) and I worked together as missionary partners in Brazil. I'm a member of a Catholic order but this was a case where some Baptists and Catholics worked together. They told me so much about you and Ron and that if I ever came through Richmond, I had to call you. I'm here for just a couple of hours and wanted to call and chat."

After filling me in on a few details, Pat paused for a thoughtful moment and said, "You know what? I really am Sister Pat and that really was Sister Ann."

Concluding Thoughts

When people know we accept them for who they are, for what they believe, and for how they do things, amazing things begin to happen. Conversation and reconciliation become possible because there is no longer the requirement for them to come over from their side to ours. There are no longer two sides but we are attempting to create a large open middle space of "different things for different people." This applies to all the dimensions of life, not just the religious or political. You don't have to do it my way to be accepted and loved. You don't have to do it my way to be my brother or sister.

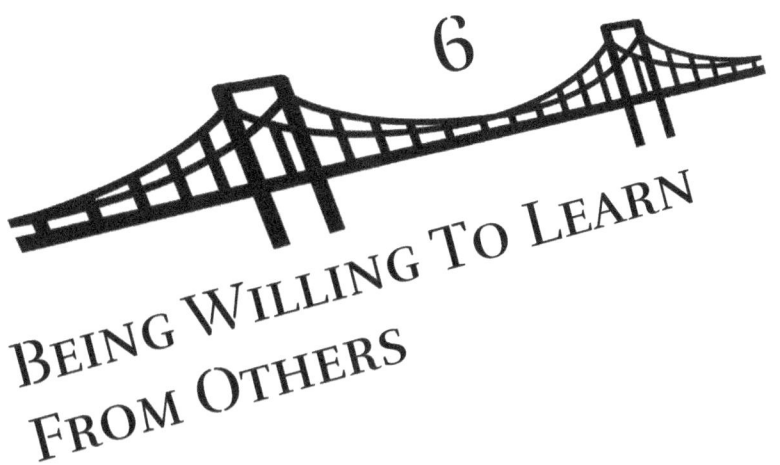

6
Being Willing To Learn From Others

Biblical Soundings

Romans 1:11-12 — *I long to see you so that I may impart to you some spiritual gift to make you strong – that is, that you and I may be mutually encouraged by each other's faith.*

(BARCLAY): *For I long to see you, because I want to share with you some of the gifts the Spirit gives, so that you and I may both be cheered and encouraged, when we meet, I by your faith and you by mine.*

Exodus 18:17-19 — *Moses' father-in-law replied, "What you are doing is not good. You and these people who come to you will only wear yourselves out. The work is too heavy for you; you cannot handle it alone."*

The Great Teacher Shows A New Face

I have forgotten the movie but I do remember the buzzer. The advertising campaign for the film promised that before any especially frightening scene, a buzzer would sound so that those who did not want to subject themselves to such terror, could close their eyes. The buzzer gave its warning before scenes that today seem mild and far from calling for blackouts. I have often felt that some of my books should provide some sort of an alert for sections that some might regard as shocking. For some, the following paragraph may fall into that category.

The text from Romans 1:11-12 provides a different side of Paul who is often charged with being dogmatic. Some of the writings attributed to him in earlier biblical translations appear to justify that conclusion. In the period during which the New Testament was written, it was not uncommon for a disciple to write in the name of his teacher or for the manuscript to remain anonymous. (None of the original Gospels had an author's name attached; they were added later.) Most scholars recognize seven Pauline epistles as from his hand: 1 Thessalonians, 1 and 2 Corinthians, Galatians, Philemon, Romans, and Philippians. Many apparent contradictions are solved when this thesis is adopted. This in no way implies that the other letters are not to be regarded as Scripture; it simply suggests that they are not from the hand of Paul. (The buzzer will now be shut off!)

Paul writes to people he does not know, in a place he has not visited, that he longs to visit them in order that they may be mutually encouraged by each other's faith. Wuest's commentary on Romans provides this insightful commentary:

> Paul guards himself against the possible appearance of underestimating that Christian standpoint of his readers, to whom he was still, personally, a stranger…. Hence he would say, "I desire to impart some spiritual gift that you may be strengthened; not that I would imply a reproach of weakness or instability, but that I desire for you the strengthening of which I stand in need along with you, and which I hope may be wrought in us both by personal intercourse and our mutual faith" (Vincent)….It is a mutual strengthening, brought about by Paul's ministry among them and their association with him, that the apostle is speaking of.[1]

---

1 Kenneth S. Wuest, *Romans* (Grand Rapids: Wm. B. Eerdmans Publishing Company, 1955), 21-22.

Who Would Be Presumptuous Enough To Correct Moses?

Exodus 18 contains some astonishing material. In 3:1, Jethro is introduced as Moses' father-in-law, the priest of Midian. In 4:18, Jethro grants Moses permission to take his family and return to Egypt. He suddenly reappears with Moses' wife and two sons (who had been sent back from Egypt) in chapter eighteen. Moses relates what God had done for the Israelites and Jethro, rather than Moses or Aaron, offers a sacrifice of thanksgiving. He is technically the leader of the worship service.

The next day Moses took his seat to serve as judge for the people, and they stood around him from morning till evening (18:13). After telling Moses that this is simply not workable, Jethro says, "*Listen now to me and I will give you some advice...*" (18:19). He instructs Moses to select capable men to serve as judges and to reserve for himself only the most difficult cases. Even Jethro's advice had an important "only if" clause: "*If you do this and God so commands, you will be able to stand the strain, and all these people will go home satisfied*" (18:23).

Here is the response of Moses: *Moses listened to his father-in-law and did everything he said"* (18:24). One commentator summarizes what has occurred: "Jethro is depicted as an efficiency expert who wisely suggests a modification in Israel's leadership structure (cf. vv. 17-23), which Moses then adopted with divine permission."[2]

Ramifications

If We Already Have The Truth...

The warm-blooded controversy had rages for fifteen years, before a new perception of dinosaurs as quick-moving, active animals was accepted – but not without lasting animos-

---

2   Frank E. Gaebelein, ed., *The Expositor's Bible Commentary*, Vol. 2 (Grand Rapids: Zondervan, 1990), 412.

ities. At conventions, there were still colleagues who did not speak to one another.[3]

One advantage of the book over the movie is that you get details that don't "move the story along" but contribute to your understanding of the broader context. Good works of fiction are not all fictional. Many historical details provide a factual framework for the development of the plot. The above quote from Michael Crichton's *Jurassic Park* provides a glimpse into the humanity of a group of scientific "experts." For years, dinosaurs were viewed as cold-blooded reptiles who went slowly lumbering about in their world. Two opinions developed, two sides emerged, and former colleagues found it unnecessary to speak to one another because already they had learned what they needed to know. As Chester A. Riley in the long-forgotten *Life of Riley* radio show frequently opined: "My head is made up!"

On the front page of the Courier-Journal this morning (October 7, 2021), there is a large photo of a school board meeting picturing people shouting at one another. The meeting had to be suspended because order could not be maintained. The issue is unimportant when placed next to the need for "rational dialogue" in the public square. I do not doubt the sincerity of those on each side of the argument. The tragedy is that neither side believes it is necessary to listen to the other side because they have nothing to learn. It is the same attitude reflected in a famous (infamous?) comment made several years ago by someone (name withheld) who was asked how he would dialogue with those who disagreed with his position. His response: "Dialogue? If you have the truth, what is there to dialogue about?"

THERE IS ALWAYS VALUE IN LISTENING TO OTHERS.

I wrote "You bet!" in the margin next to this quote:

> An education which teaches about and values the views of others different from ourselves can also be transformative.

---

3   Michael Crichton, *Jurassic Park*, 86.

An education in which we meet and work with people who are different from us can also be. It is hard to be prejudiced against a group when you understand their views, their history, and especially know some of their members. Though very difficult, we probably need to promote dialog with those with whom we disagree.[4]

Segregation based on similar ideas and beliefs has always been a part of every culture but appears to be especially prevalent in ours. Those with opposing concepts are quite evidently not welcome and any hope for conversation is non-existent. Defending beliefs means allowing no opposing thoughts ever to be heard. Reading the right books, listening to the right people, tuning to the right media presenters, and turning a deaf ear to any contrary opinions all are part of this separation. I always have to place a disclaimer about the books that appear in the bibliography. It has been my experience, that even from writers with whom I disagree on most things, I have found some new insights, perspectives, and questions. Citing references does not mean I concur with everything an author says. I agree with Steven Klees: I need to be in dialog with those with whom I disagree. I have found many of those dialogues transformative.

> Those who teach religion and preach the truths of faith to an unbelieving world are perhaps more concerned with proving themselves right than with really discovering and satisfying the spiritual hunger of those to whom they speak. Again, we are too ready to assume that we know, better than the unbeliever, what ails him…We do not realize that he is listening not for words but for the evidence of thought and love behind the words. Yet if he is not instantly converted by our sermons, we console ourselves with the thought that this is due to his fundamental perversity.
>
> …we must first try to find out what they need, and perhaps also we might devote a little more thought to the question

---

4   Steven Klees, *The Conscience of a Progressive*, 155.

whether it is not possible that, in a dialogue with them, they might have something to give to us.[5]

In what I consider to be Merton's classic on reconciliation and bridgebuilding, the above selection from *Passion for Peace* is the prescription for reaching out to people where they are. Too many assumptions are made about what people think, how they feel, what they need, and how they see us. None of this information is available secondhand. If they don't tell us, we don't know. And if they don't tell us we don't know them and we don't know the best way to have a conversation with them. I know from experience, that if people perceive that we believe they have something to give us, new avenues for communication open up. Merton goes so far as to say, "A test of our sincerity in the practice of nonviolence is this: are we willing to learn something from our adversary?"[6]

As far as I am concerned, the classic line in the movie *Harvey* comes when someone asks Elwood P. Dowd, "May I help you?" The reply is: "What did you have in mind?" What is it that we have in mind when we try to build bridges of reconciliation? Do we simply want people to believe the way we do, behave the way we do, adopt the culture we have, view life with the same perspectives, and become like us? The old cliché comes to mind: "A know it all is especially offensive to those of us who do." If we are a "know it all," I don't believe anyone will want to walk across any bridges with us.

THINKING OF IT IN A NEW WAY

> When the Wright brothers said they thought together, what they really meant is that they fought together. Arguing was the family business. Although their father was a bishop in a local church, he included books by atheists in his library – and encouraged his children to read and debate them.
>
> "Honest argument is merely a process of mutually picking the beams and motes out of each other's eyes so both

---

5 Thomas Merton, *Passion for Peace* (New York: Crossroad, 1996), 140.
6 Ibid, 255.

Building Bridges in a World of Crumbling Connections 59

can see clearly," Wilbur once wrote to a colleague whose ego was bruised after a fiery exchange about aeronautics. Wilbur stressed that it wasn't personal: he saw arguments as opportunities to test and refine their thinking.[7]

Currently I am reading a book about the life and times of Mary Ball Washington, the mother of George Washington.[8] The book is filled the discussions, arguments, shouting matches, and total disagreements that characterized many of the efforts to forge a new kind of government for the thirteen colonies. Rather than get discouraged over what chaos this must have been, we need to remember that, out of these mayhem sessions, came the Constitution, the Bill of Rights, and George Washington as our first president. It helps to see these free for all meetings "as opportunities to test and refine their thinking."

How Lafayette Made The Connection With Washington

You think you know something about one of history's memorable moments until someone takes you there in a new way. Such has been my experience in reading *Valley Forge* by Bob Drury and Tom Clavin.[9] On the back cover, two reviewers, Lynn Vincent and Sara Vladic, write: "In these pages, Bob Drury and Tom Clavin, masters of narrative nonfiction, whisk us into a pivotal moment in American history." They are right. I feel that I am experiencing the events surrounding Valley Forge in an entirely new way, especially in my appreciation for Lafayette. If you want a book that will be a bridge for your appreciation of reading history, this is my highly recommended place to begin.

In 1777, the wealthy young French nobleman who volunteered to serve in the army without compensation, was only nineteen

---

7   Adam Grant, *Think Again*, 81, 92.
8   Craig Shirley, *Mary Ball Washington* (New York: Harper, 2019).
9   Bob Drury and Tom Clavin, *Valley Forge* (New York: Simon and Schuster, 2018), back cover.

when he met Washington. One paragraph speaks volumes to the thesis of this chapter:

> In Layette, however, (Washington) had discovered an officer from a lofty and professional European army who proffered not only respect but subservience of rank to the diffident former member of Virginia's middle gentry. Upon their initial inspection of the Continental Army, for instance, Washington's old insecurities surfaced when he apologized to Lafayette for the threadbare clothing and substandard armaments of his troops. Without hesitation the Frenchman replied that he had come to the United States to learn from the Americans, and not to teach. Washington never forgot the moment.[10]

On their very first meeting, the authors give a novel-like feel to the encounter:

> Lafayette charmed Washington with his youthful brio for poetic pronouncements as well as his ability to segue from diffident self-abasement to fervent ambition in mid-sentence. Adding to his cachet was his physical stature. In an era when men's average height was five feet four inches, the young Frenchman could directly meet the gaze of the Continental Army's commander in chief.[11]

Perhaps my favorite touch in Lafayette's bridge-building is this:

> Many of Lafayette's detractors, descended from good Puritan stock, found off-putting his gallic habit of hugging people at the slightest provocation. Throughout his life, Washington had always shied away from any physical familiarity, instant or deliberate…. Yet there was something about Lafayette that penetrated the commander in chief's hard shell.[12]

This is a connection that brought a lot of mutual learning at one of the most crucial times in American history.

---

10 Ibid, 31.
11 Ibid, 29.
12 Ibid, 31.

The Goal Is Lifelong Learning

> A mark of lifelong learners is recognizing that they can learn something from everyone they meet.… Arrogance leaves us blind to our weaknesses. Humility is a reflective lens: it helps us see them clearly. Confident humility is a corrective lens: it enables us to overcome those weaknesses.[13]

Pharrell Adams said, "If you're not learning, you're wasting your time."[14] I remember once hearing a sermon with the title, "Are You On the Grow?" I can't imagine reaching the point in life where one can say, "I have nothing else to learn." Many teachers contend that the mark of true wisdom is the realization of just how much there is that we don't know. Jesus called "disciples" (a much better translation is "learners") and I don't read anywhere that he ever gave them a diploma. None of them ever graduated. The school of discipleship we enter has never had a graduating class because the learning never stops and the growing never ceases. Furthermore, I am convinced that we enter the next life at the level on which we leave this one and continue with our learning.

Alex Beard gives a "Manifesto for Learning." Here are a few of the highlights (each is unpacked in detail in the book):[15]

1. Learn forever. Self-motivation is the key. George Saunders urges, "Stay so open it hurts."
2. Think critically. Misinformation erodes our shared culture. There are no shortcuts. If it feels easy, then we're avoiding real thought.
3. Get creative. Most of us went to schools where we made art, performed in plays, carried out science experiments, indulged our curiosity, but not today, our kids are missing out on these experiences.
4. Develop character.

---
13 Adam Grant, *Think Again,* 54.
14 Alex Beard, *Natural Born Learners* (London: Weidenfeld and Nicolson, 2018), 297.
15 Ibid, 299-307.

5. Start early.
6. Grow co-operation. Generation Me is giving way to Generation Us...Instead of figuring out "Who is the best?", we might ask, "What might we be able to offer each other?" and "How best can we work together?"
7. Practice Teaching.
8. Use technology wisely. The robot teachers aren't coming yet. Technology is just that, a tool. Human plus machine plus better process wins.
9. Build the future

CONCLUDING THOUGHTS

Leatherbound books are an expensive form of wallpaper, and yet every English nobleman's home seems to have them. Their endless sets of the works of Cooper and Scott and Goethe, in finely tanned bindings with marbled endpapers, all end up with (a book) dealer sooner or later. I look through a set of Cooper and, without surprise, find uncut pages: these books were never actually read.[16]

The above comes from a novel with the subtitle: "*Lost in a Town of Books.*" It is set in Wales in Hay-on-Wye, a town that has fifteen hundred inhabitants, five churches, four grocers, two newsagents, one post office...and forty bookstores.[17] The quote I selected for inclusion brings to mind a question: I wonder how many uncut pages of valuable learning we have in our lives that remain "on the shelf"? There is so much yet to be discovered and much of it in some of the most unlikely places and from the most unlikely people.

---

16 Paul Collins, *Sixpence House* (New York: Bloomsbury, 2003), 17.
17 Ibid, 22.

Giving Up The Joys Of Judgment

Biblical Soundings

Matthew 7:1-5 — *"Do not judge, or you too will be judged. For in the same way you judge others, you will be judged, and with the measure you use, it will be measured to you.*

"Why do you look at the speck of sawdust in someone else's eye and pay no attention to the plank in your own eye? How can you say, 'Let me take the speck out of your eye,' when all the time there is a plank in your own eye? You hypocrite, first take the plank out of your own eye, and then you will see clearly to remove the speck for the other person's eye."

Romans 14:3, 5, 10, 13 — *The one who eats everything must not treat with contempt the one who does not, and the one who does not eat everything must not judge the one who does, for God has accepted that person.*

Some consider one day more sacred than another; others, consider every day alike. Everyone should be fully convinced in their own mind.

You, then, why do you judge your brother or sister? Or why do you treat your brother or sister with contempt? For we will all stand before God's judgment seat.

Therefore let us stop passing judgment on one another.

Luke 9:51b-56 — *Jesus resolutely set out for Jerusalem. And he sent messengers on ahead, who went into a Samaritan village to get things ready for him; but the people did not welcome him, because he was heading for Jerusalem. When the disciples James and John saw this, they asked, "Lord, do you want us to call fire down from heaven to destroy them?" but Jesus turned and rebuked them. Then he and his disciples went to another village.*

GIVE UP BEING CRITIC AT LARGE.

In Matthew 7:1, Jesus is not talking about the necessary judgments that are part of our integrity and morality. (The unpacking of this would require another book.) Many modern translations capture the meaning of the Greek text:

BARCLAY: *Don't make a habit of judging others, if you do not want to be judged yourself.*

WUEST: *Stop pronouncing censorious criticism, in order that you may not be the object of censorious criticism....*

Clearly, Jesus is calling for us not to be critical persons. The critical life stance is most developed in those who have, what I like to call, "speck-tacular" vision; they can spot a speck from a mile away. This simply kicks off mutual judgment with its inherent damage to relationships (not to mention self-esteem). Speck hunting expeditions keep us unaware of the plank (other translations have "log") in our own eye. Other-awareness replaces self-awareness. We not only create a barrier with the other person, we have created a barrier with ourselves. We have become what most translations term "a hypocrite." The literal meaning of that word is spelled out in WUEST: *O actor on the stage of life, draw out first from your eye the log, and then you will see clearly to draw out the splinter from the eye of your brother* (7:5). We are playing a part that does not belong to us. The basic biblical teaching found everywhere in Scripture is: God is the judge, we are not.

Perhaps the most damaging part of playing this role is that our vision is distorted by what we do not realize is in our own eye.

We are unable to see clearly the other person and we are unable to clearly see ourselves. This is a basic reality distortion that lies at the root of so many prejudices and demeaning of others whom we see as less (more flawed) than ourselves. The place to begin with fault-finding is with ourselves. I quickly confess that as I have gotten older and am more fully aware of the many logs I have to deal with, I have far less time (and much less incentive) to deal with my "splintered" friends. It's all a matter of where I believe God wants me to begin in dealing with what is wrong in the world.

Faith Convictions Have Varied From The Beginning.

In Romans 14, Paul deals with two issues that seem foreign to most of us and the specifics of which we do not know. "Diet practices differ and the differences are bound to be observed; they become a topic of conversation and a basis of disagreement.... Whether the question of regarding one day as more sacred than another refers to Sabbath observance or to special days for feasting or fasting is not easily determined."[1]

The problem is that these issues have become the bases for judgment and disruption in the faith community, even to the point of treating others with contempt (14:3). Paul's "solution" to the problem is that the judging should stop with the recognition of two principles: everyone should be fully convinced in their own mind as to their practice (vs. 5) and we will all give an account of ourselves to God, not to one another (vs. 12). Who are we to be judging? Ultimately, we are not going to be the judges, but the judged.

Violence Can Quickly Come On The Heels Of Judgment

The Thunder brothers ask if it would be okay to add a little lighting to their stormy dispositions. Remember: Mark 3:17 tells us that James and John were known as the "sons of thunder" when

---

1 Frank E. Gaebelein, ed., *The Expositor's Bible Commentary*, Vol. 10 (Grand Rapids: Zondervan, 1976), 144 – 145.

Jesus called them to be his disciples. We are not told how they came to earn that title, but the episode in Luke 9:51-56 gives a hint of how the tag might have been put on them. Jesus' rejection for nightly lodging by a Samaritan village is all it takes to bring long-standing animosity to the surface.

> The history of the Samaritans is uncertain. Many hold that they were a mixed-race since the fall of the northern kingdom of Israel. The king of Assyria deported the leaders of Israel, among them the religious teachers, replacing them with foreigners….Some think that the Samaritans known in the NT arose in the early Hellenistic period….Being semipagan, the Samaritans were a fringe segment of the Jewish world for which Jesus, and Luke following him, had a concern. They are not mentioned unfavorably elsewhere in Luke; on the contrary, he mentions them favorably in 10:30-37 and 17:11-19.[2]

Regardless of origin, the major bone of contention was the location for the proper place of worship. The Samaritans worshiped on Mount Gerizim and rejected Jerusalem. This issue is one Jesus discusses in John 4:19-24 in the "Samaritan woman at the well" episode. The Gospel writer also includes (usually placed in parenthesis) the commentary: *"Jews did not associate with Samaritans"* *(John 4:9).*

Ramifications

Not A Bad Place To Begin

> Mary made sure that Washington was a frequent visitor at Mount Vernon, and thus also at Belvoir, where he could observe elite masculinity up close. Washington supplemented his fieldwork by studying *Rules of Civility and Decent Behaviour in Company and Conversation,* a sixteenth-century book on

---

2 Frank E. Gaebelein, *The Expositors Bible Commentary,* Vol 8 (Grand Rapids: Zondervan, 1984), 933.

etiquette. He likely copied down all 110 lessons merely to work on his penmanship....[3]

Much has been written (and debated) about the relationship between George Washington and his mother, Mary Ball Washington. As a very young man, it is evident his mother made every effort to provide the kind of education that many biographers believe helped to make Washington our first truly national hero and celebrity. As a widowed mother, she wanted him to be a man's man. Throughout his years of military service, the troops not only respected him, their affection for him was never in doubt. Instead of "critic at large," I think of Washington as "enabler at large." One of the rules of civility in the book on etiquette cited above was: "Associate yourself with men of good quality if you esteem your own reputation, for 'tis better to be alone than in bad company."[4] Washington took the first logical step in following this rule: he became one of those men of good quality himself.

Becoming the "best versions of ourselves" is the first step in becoming a non-judgmental person. Jesus' primary emphasis on the kind of persons we are, is revealed in the Sermon on the Mount: *"Every good tree bears good fruit, but a bad tree bears bad fruit. A good tree cannot bear bad fruit, and a bad tree cannot bear good fruit"* (Matthew 7:17-18). Practicing civility and decent behavior in company and conversation will set us on the path to becoming the kind of persons who have more important things to attend to than looking for flaws in the lives of those around them. My observation has been that I have never met anyone who liked a judgmental person. The fault-finders and critics are never found on favorite-person lists. Washington was admired and loved because he was truly of noble character. His attitude, speech, and actions revealed traits that brought admiration and led to his being the only president ever unanimously nominated by the electors.

---

3   Alexis Coe, *You Never Forget Your First* (New York: Penguin Books, 2020), 6.
4   Ibid.

The Way We Usually Judge Is Highly-Flawed

> "Isn't it extraordinary?" Ed Regis said. "Especially on a misty day, these plants really contribute to the prehistoric atmosphere. These are authentic Jurassic ferns, of course."
> Ellie paused to look closely at the ferns. Whoever had decided to place this particular fern at poolside obviously didn't know that the spores of *veriformans* contained a deadly beta-carboline alkaloid. Even touching the attractive green fronds could make you sick....They just chose plants for appearance, as they would choose a picture for the wall. It never occurred to them that plants were actually living things, busily performing all the living functions of respiration, ingestion, excretion, reproduction – and defense.[5] (My comment in the margin: And so with humans!)

"Don't judge a book by its cover," has a much larger application. It is so easy to make an immediate assessment of an individual simply by appearance. We all have certain built-in criteria that provide the bases for our judgments. One frequently heard cliché is, "You know how _____ are." Place in that blank any group you can think of. When someone says, "You know how ministers are," my response is: "No I don't. I know something about how particular ministers are but I can't think of any characteristic that will lump them all together." Choosing a plant because it looks good only makes further homework necessary. Judging people because of an appealing trait or physical attribute is no basis for sound evaluation.

David McRaney has a section in his book, *You Are Now Less Dumb*, in which he discusses the "halo effect." That is when "you judge specific qualities of others based on your global evaluation of their character and appearance."[6] Because all heroes were perceived as naturally tall, that became a problem for short actors who were playing heroes. Hollywood solved the problem with "special shoes, low camera angles, and specially constructed out-of-proportion

---

5 Michael Creighton, *Jurassic Park,* 87.
6 David McRaney, *You Are Now Less Dumb* (New York: Gotham Books, 2013), 83.

door frames. They even dug long trenches in which the other people in a scene walked alongside the leading man while the camera was running."[7] My favorite remedy for "shortness" was called the "apple box solution." The man simple stood on an apple box when among taller cast members. "They sometimes called apple boxes "man makers."[8] Appearances can not only be deceiving, they can also be manipulating. They can make us see something that isn't true. We then judge on the basis of something that isn't there.

THE BASIC REASON WE SHOULD NOT JUDGE

> In his later work Bernard Lonergan formulated an understanding of faith as "a new knowledge born of love" in *Method in Theology*. Lonergan also wrote a book on a new theory of economics, which has been praised by several economists but which I am not competent to judge.[9]

If you ever want to read someone who will keep you on your intellectual toes (it kept me consulting the dictionary and books on Greek mythology), it is David Tracy. *Filaments* is heavy plowing but well worth the effort. I welcome his wisdom because of his wealth of knowledge. I respect him as a scholar because when he mentions Lonergan's book on economics he writes: "I am not competent to judge." I would love to make a bumper sticker out of these words because that is the basic reason we should not spend our time judging others: we are not competent to do so. We do not have sufficient information; we do not know motives or intentions; we do not know enough about the life story; we do not have information on present crises through which the person is passing; we do not know what battles they are fighting; we do not know how things look from their perspective. This is just a representative list of things we do not know.

---

7   Ibid, 84.
8   Ibid.
9   David Tracy, *Filaments* (Chicago: The University of Chicago Press, 2020), 191.

I remember with trembling my year of teaching at a Junior High School. I had taken the required education course in college, done my "practice teaching," and had my teaching certificate in hand. None of these had prepared me for the challenges offered by the Junior High experience. My inexperience didn't help the situation either. One English class I taught proved the most difficult. I did my best at attempting to interest the teenagers in the rules of grammar and the diagramming of sentences. (I don't think that is now done because hardly anyone seems to know the difference between the nominative and objective cases. Hence, we hear, "He threw a party for Frank and I.") One student in the class was especially disruptive and I tried everything in my power to get her attention and calm her down. In the faculty lounge one day, I was in a rant about Mary (not her real name) when one of the other teachers asked, "Do you know anything about her?" My too quick reply was, "I already know more than I want to know." That is never true when you teach. The teacher continued: "Mary is the oldest of three children and comes from a home where the father abandoned them and the mother is an alcoholic. Each morning, she makes breakfast for her two younger sisters, gets them ready for school, packs their lunches, and gets them on the school bus."

The next time the class met and I saw Mary, I was looking at an entirely different person. My methods changed because my attitude changed. Years later, I was to preach a sermon titled: "The First Word in God's Vocabulary is not Judgment, but Mercy" based on Luke 6:36: *Be merciful, just as you Father is merciful.*" In the sermon, I asked which we would prefer when this life is over: judgment or mercy?

"Mercy" is always the answer and you don't even have to read Psalm 130:4 to know that: *If you, Lord, kept a record of sins, Lord, who could stand?* Before God gives Moses the commandments for the second time (Moses smashed the first tablets when he came down from the mountain and saw the golden calf party), the Lord speaks these words about himself: *The Lord, the Lord, a God merciful and gracious, slow to anger, and abounding in steadfast love and faith-*

fulness, keeping steadfast love for the thousandth generation, forgiving iniquity and transgressing and sin…(Exodus 34:6-7a).

Mercy is God's first word; it is also his last word.

CONCLUDING THOUGHTS

Romans 2:16 - *This will take place on the day when God judges everyone's secrets through Jesus Christ, as my gospel declares.* Frederick Buechner, in commenting on this verse writes: "There will come a Day on which all our days and all the judgments upon us and all our judgments upon each other will themselves be judged. The judge will be Christ. In other words, the one who judges us most finally will be the one who loves us most fully."[10] I added my line: This is the one who knows us most fully and is qualified to deal with all our secrets. How grateful I am that this is the one who loves us most fully.

---

10 Dallas Willard, et al., *Faith That Matters* (New York: HarperOne, 2018), 123.

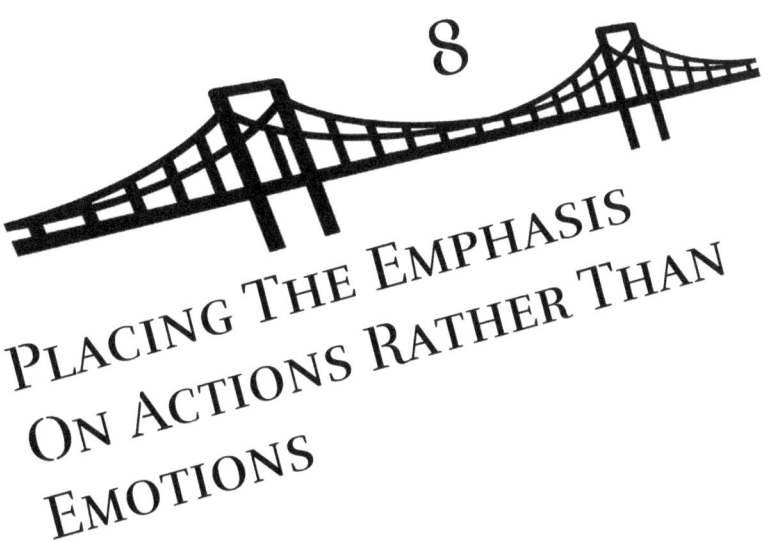

8

Placing The Emphasis On Actions Rather Than Emotions

Biblical Soundings

Matthew 7:24 — *Therefore everyone who hears these word of mine and puts them into practice is like a wise man who built his house on the rock.*

(WUEST) *Therefore, everyone who is of such a character as to be habitually hearing these words of mine and habitually doing them, shall be likened to an intelligent man who is of such a nature that he built his house upon the rocky cliff.*

James 2:14-19 — *What good is it, my brothers and sisters, if people claim to have faith but have no deeds? Can faith save them? Suppose a brother or sister is without clothes and daily food. If one of you says to them, "Go in peace; keep warm and well fed," but does nothing about their physical needs, what good is it? In the same way, faith by itself, if it is not accompanied by action, is dead.*

But someone will say, "You have faith; I have deeds." Show me your faith without deeds, and I will show you my faith by what I do. You believe there is one God. Good! Even the demons believe that – and shudder. (The reference in this last verse is to Deuteronomy 6:4).

BARCLAY: *If faith does not issue in action, if it is all alone by itself, it is dead (2:17).*

1 Corinthians 13:4-7 — *Love is patient, love is kind. It does not envy, it does not boast, it is not proud. It does not dishonor others, it is not self-seeking, it is not easily angered, it keeps no record of wrongs. Love does not delight in evil but rejoice with the truth. It always protects, always trusts, always hopes, always perseveres.*

1 Corinthians 13:4b 8 (WUEST) — *Love is kind, gentle, benign, pervading and penetrating the whole nature, mellowing all which would have been harsh and austere; is not envious. Love does not brag, nor does it show itself off, is not ostentatious, does not have an inflated ego, does not act unbecomingly, does not seek after the things which are its own, is not irritated, provoked, exasperated, aroused to anger, does not take into account the evil (which it suffers), does not rejoice at the iniquity but rejoices with the truth, endures all things, believes all things, hopes all things, bears up under all things, not losing heart nor courage. Love never fails.*

When you read the gospel of Matthew, you quickly discover that Jesus is presented as the great Teacher. Many commentators have called Matthew the teaching Gospel. An obvious feature of Matthew's structure that distinguishes it from Mark, is the author's arrangement of the teaching material in five great discourses, each of which concludes with the formula "And when Jesus finished these sayings" (7:21, 11;1; 13:53, 19:1; 26:1)....Because these discourses are obviously of great importance to Matthew, it has been proposed that his intention was to compose a new "Pentateuch" modeled on the Five Books of Moses....[1]

Even those not familiar with the Bible know something about what we call the Sermon on the Mount (Matthew 5 – 7). I agree with William Barclay's assessment:

> We speak of the Sermon on the Mount as if it was one single sermon preached on a single occasion. But it is far more

---

[1] Douglas R. A. Hare, Matthew: Interpretation (Louisville: John Knox Press, 1993), 2.

than that there are good and compelling and convincing reasons for thinking that the Sermon on the Mount is far more than one sermon, that it is, in fact, a kind of epitome of all the sermons Jesus ever preached.[2]

Barclay gives two possible translations of Matthew 5:1 to underscore this thesis:

> *When Jesus saw the crowds, He went up into the mountain; and when He had sat down, His disciples came to Him; and when He had opened His mouth, this is what He used to teach them.*[3]

He opened his mind and heart to them, and this was the substance of his teaching.[4]

Matthew 5 – 7 is the best biblical summary I know that answers the question, "What did Jesus teach?" It also answers the question, "What does a follower of Jesus look like?" It's really a job description. (More about what this means in the Ramifications section.) It still puzzles me that so many want the Ten Commandments posted in various places and appear to ignore the ramifications and specificity of the Sermon on the Mount as it applies to conduct in the public square. Matthew portrays Jesus as the new Moses.

> In Exodus, God calls Moses to ascend Mount Sinai to receive the law. Mount Sinai was wrapped in smoke, and the whole mountain throbbed with the presence of God and the thunder of his voice. The Lord summoned Moses to join him on the mountain, warning that no others, except Aaron, were permitted to accompany Moses up the mountain (Exodus 19:16-25) It is, therefore, remarkable that the disciples had the courage to join Jesus on the mountain in order to receive his teaching. Jesus, the new Moses, is surrounded by his disciples so that they may be taught, as Israel was taught by Moses, to be holy.

---

2 William Barclay, The Gospel of Matthew, Vol 1, 79.
3 Ibid, 81.
4 William Barclay, The New Testament (Louisville: Westminster John Knox Press, 1999).

Matthew does not suggest that Jesus addresses only the disciples from the mountain. We are told that he "taught them," which may indicate that he taught those in the crowd as well as the disciples.[5]

John 1:16: Codicil to Sermon on the Mount: *For the law was given through Moses; grace and truth came through Jesus Christ.* The Sermon on the Mount is not like the Ten Words engraved on tablets of stone. The Sermon on the Mount cannot be separated from its teacher; the prologue (John 1:1-18) was never meant to be separated from the giver of grace and truth. Although I believe the sermon is the description of Kingdom citizens, it is not something that has to be achieved in order to be accepted; it is part of that truth that the Spirit continues to lead us into. We have the challenge and the ideals of Matthew 5 – 7 in the context of grace and truth that already belong to us and in which we stand. The same kind of love, acceptance, and forgiveness that brought us into the Kingdom continue to be the things we want to be a part of our lives because of what we have already received and because of who we already are – God's children.

Martin Luther may have felt that James was a "rather strawy epistle," but I contend it is a necessary epistle to keep us from building our lives out of straw. Our text from James clearly echoes: "A 'faith' which is purely doctrinal and does not result in pious action (i.e. charity) is a dead sham, totally useless for salvation. True faith reveals itself in pious deeds of love, as the examples of Abraham and Rahab show."[6]

Paul's great chapter on love is a classic illustration of the principle. When he wants to describe what he means by "the greatest thing in the world," (1 Corinthians 13:13), he doesn't use adjectives, he uses verbs. Many sermons have been preached on the

---

5   Stanley Hauerwas, Matthew (Grand Rapids: Brazos Press, 2006), 58.
6   Peter Davids, *Commentary on James: New International Greek Testament Commentary* (Grand Rapids: Wm. B. Eerdmans Publishing Co., 1983), 119.

subject "Love Is a Verb." Paul doesn't describe how love feels, he describes what love does. We'll deal shortly with how this enables us to love our enemies.

RAMIFICATIONS

FAITH AS A VERB

The English language handicaps us when we try to speak of faith. It gives us no verb form of the word. As we have seen, the Greek verb *pistuo* and the Latin verb *credo* permitted writers and speakers to say, "I trust, I commit myself, I rest my heart upon, I pledge allegiance." All of these paraphrases show us that faith is a *verb*. It is an active mode of being and committing, a way of moving into and giving shape to our experiences of life. They also show us that faith is always *relational*, there is always *another* in faith. "I trust in and am loyal to…"[7]

In my last book, *Faith Never Stands Alone*, I attempt to rescue the word from the understanding of faith as simply those things we believe. In the above excerpt, James Fowler makes the case for what I believe is the essence of biblical teaching: faith is a verb. In his excellent book, *Nine Essential Things I've Learned About Life*, Rabbi Harold Kushner has a chapter titled: "Religion is What You Do, Not What You Believe."[8]

I don't think it was by accident that Christians were first called "Followers of the Way." Jesus begins the parable that ends the Sermon on the Mount with: *Everyone who hears these words of mine and DOES them….*(Matthew 7:24). The sermon also explains what it means to be the "light of the world": *Let your light so shine before others, so that they may SEE YOUR GOOD WORKS and give glory to your Father in heaven"* (NRSV). Morton Kelsey gives this summary

---
7   James Fowler, *Stages of Faith* (New York: HarperOne, 1981), 16.
8   Harold Kushner, Nine Essential Things I've Learned About Life (New York: Anchor Books, 2015), 103f.

statement: "Remember also that what we do is a better indication of what we believe than what we think we think."[9]

At a 1985 summer seminar, I heard a professor relate a story I have never forgotten. He had gone to India the previous year to see firsthand and photograph some of the work of Mother Teresa in Calcutta. In the fall, he gave a talk to his students and showed them some of the slides he had taken. Following his presentation, he asked if anyone had a question. One student asked: "Does Mother Teresa ever give her Christian testimony?" I have forgotten his reply but I think I know how I would have responded. Some of John's disciples have been sent by their teacher to ask Jesus: *"Are you the one who to come, or should we expect someone else?" Jesus replied, "Go back and report to John what you hear and see: The blind receive sight, the lame walk, and those who have leprosy are cleansed, the deaf hear, the dead are raised, and the good news is proclaimed to the poor"* (Matthew 11:2-5).

IT HAS TO BE SEEN AND HEARD

From the Metropolitan Diary section of the New York Times:

> The supermarket clerk was obviously in a bad mood, and Jerome Coppersmith was surprised by her actions – mishandling groceries and snatching the money from customers' hands. The elderly man in front of him, who had just sampled her rudeness, looked at the clerk as he awaited his change. "Aren't you going to tell me to have a nice day?" he asked. "I don't have to," she snapped. "It's on the receipt."

I can only imagine the speechless customer taking his groceries and leaving in amazement. Perhaps it takes an extreme example to remind us that our faith, our set of beliefs, cannot be something that is simply in our hearts and minds or printed in our prayer books. Building a bridge to such a disgruntled worker is no easy task. I'm going to suggest some of the responses I would have been

---

9   Morton Kelsey, Companions on the Inner Way (New York: Crossroad, 1983), 14.

tempted to make: "Well, I'm sorry you don't seem to be having a very nice day, but I sincerely hope things get better as time goes on"; "It may be on the receipt, but it always makes me feel good to hear those words spoken, especially if I'm having a not-so-good day"; "Well, I hope you will feel like telling others. Later, there may be someone in your line who desperately needs to hear it because they haven't heard a kind word all day."

The consistent movement of the Christian faith from an insignificant corner of the world to the halls of power in the Roman Empire has always seemed to me a miracle of the first order. David Bentley Hart offers his explanation for how this happened:

> It is…wise to recall that the Christians of the early centuries won renown principally for their sobriety, peacefulness, generosity, loyalty to their spouses, care for the poor and the sick, and ability, no matter what their social station to exhibit virtues – self-restraint, chastity, forbearance, courage – that pagan philosophers frequently extolled but rarely practiced with comparable fidelity. And these Christians brought something new into the ancient world; a vision of the good with precedent in pagan society, a creed that prescribed charitable service to others as a *religious* obligation, a story about a God of self-outpouring love.[10]

AND THE CHANGES WILL COME

I have always believed that others change in response to the changes we make in our own behavior (words and deeds). One writer carries this idea a step further:

> Act first. Think later. We need to do first and reflect afterwards. Life isn't always about logical planning – it's about lived experiences that challenge our assumptions and offer a route to insight and self-discovery.[11]

---

[10] David Bentley Hart, *Atheist Delusions* (New Haven: Yale University Press, 2009), 45.
[11] Roman Krznaric, *Carpe Diem Regained* (London: Unbound, 2017), 8.

Too many of my plans never got off the drawing board. I wanted to make sure I had thought it all out before I took any action. Of course, planning is necessary but, I'll have to confess, with all my planning, many of the things I finally attempted to accomplish had twists and turns that changed almost everything about how I handled them. We learn from experience and experience comes from doing, even if that doing involves mistakes. "You've got to allow yourself to make lots of mistakes. Then the real magic will happen. If you play it really safe, you won't get any treats."[12] Insights and self-discovery, along with the real magic, come when we are not afraid to make mistakes as we attempt what we really believe we should be doing. Most of us will confess that we have learned the most, and made the most changes, as a result of our mistakes. Yes, that is where the treats come from!

Michael J. Fox found this to be true in his efforts to control Parkinson's:

> I found a movement disorder specialist, Dr. Susan Bressmen, who completely reconfigured my pharmaceutical approach toward treating Parkinson's. She also put an emphasis on physical therapy, diet, and fitness. This was restorative, less stressful, and allowed me to get a better grip on the disease.[13]

You might title this approach "from pills to action" or "from passive to active therapy" or "from easy-going therapy to hard-work responsibility." I wonder how many of us could profit from a "movement disorder specialist"? Sedentary aging is too often the preferred method for dealing with the aches and pains that accompany the piling up of the years. Every single book I have read on how to deal with the aging process always has this rejoinder: "Keep moving!"

There are far too many books on the market that carry the word "Easy" in the title. The only thing I have ever found to be easy is going downhill (physically and metaphorically). Stephen

---

12 Emily Gosling, *Great Minds Don't Think Alike*, 64.
13 Michael J. Fox, *No Time Like the Future* (New York: Flatiron Books, 2020), 22.

King is a prolific writer who had already completed five novels by his junior year in college. King shares his secret:

> (Stephen King) stresses that good writing is the product of hard work, dedication, and striving to master the items that make up a novelist's "toolbox": vocabulary, grammar, and elements of style. How to find these? Just keep on writing and reading; then writing and reading some more. There is no such thing as a muse, he says, but "you have to do all the grunt work."[14]

I have never read of any individual in any field of endeavor who has achieved what we would call success without the single magic ingredient: hard work! Do you think this might also apply to such things in our Christian faith as being ministers of reconciliation and bridge builders? In the TNIV of the letter to the churches of Galatia, there is a section headed "Doing Good to All." Perhaps the most important verse in that section is this one (Galatians 6:9): *Let us not become weary in doing good, for at the proper time we will reap a harvest if we do not give up."* Even our "doing good" involves grunt work!

> He (Dylan Wiliam) believed that the flaw in teacher training to date was that it was focused too much on knowledge and too little on practice....Changing what teachers do is more important than changing what teachers know.[15]

For ten years I taught a "Practice of Ministry" course in our local seminary. It met for two hours once a week. It was usually taken in the senior year. The irony is that most ministers experience difficulties or failure not because of a lack of knowledge but because of inadequacies or misconceptions in the practice of ministry. This "nuts and bolts" course covered such items as making and keeping a personal budget, managing time effectively, planning for continuing education, conducting weddings and funerals, pastoral visitation, community and ecumenical relationships, and how to

---

14 Emily Gosling, *Great Minds Don't Think Alike*, 105.
15 Alex Beard, *Natural Born Learners*, 168-169.

facilitate better meetings. Other items were included in this emphasis on the "doing" rather than the "thinking" in ministry.

When we began the session on how to construct a budget, one student spoke up: "I really don't need a budget because I don't have any money!" I graciously dealt with that one and explained that ministers are notoriously poor money managers. That session was always a lively, but absolutely necessary one. I never presented myself as the expert, only as one who had made enough mistakes in the "to do" department to know that I continued to be "under construction." And the most important part of my "doing" in all my years of ministry turned out to be the task of reconciliation and building (and repairing) bridges. My "relational" theology turned out to be more difficult than I ever imagined. It required a lot of hard work even (especially?) among "God's people."

CONCLUDING THOUGHTS

Atul Gawande tells of a doctor in a nursing home who persuaded the administration to bring in dogs, cats, parakeets, a colony of rabbits, and even a group of laying hens to be cared for by the residents. "The residents began to wake up and come to life. People who we had believed weren't able to speak started speaking....People who had been completely withdrawn and non-ambulatory started coming to the nurses' station and saying, 'I'll take the dog for a walk.'"[16]

---

16 Timothy Keller, *Making Sense of God* (New York: Viking, 2016), 58.

Acknowledging No Limits to God's Love and Grace

Biblical Soundings

John 1:14 — *The Word became flesh and made his dwelling among us. We have seen his glory, the glory of the one and only Son, who came from the Father, full of grace and truth.*

Luke 4:25-27 — *I assure you that there were many widows in Israel in Elijah's time, when the sky was shut for three and a half years and there was a severe famine throughout the land. Yet Elijah was not sent to any of them, but to a widow in Zarephath in the region of Sidon. And there were men in Israel with leprosy in the time of Elisha the prophet, yet not one of them was cleansed – only Naaman the Syrian.*

Romans 5:15, 20 — *But the gift is not like the trespass of the one man, how much more did God's grace and the gift that came by the grace of the one man, Jesus Christ, overflow to the many!*

Where sin increased, grace increased all the more.....

Ephesians 2:6-7 —*...in order that he might show the incomparable riches of his grace, expressed in his kindness to us in Christ Jesus. For it is by grace you have been saved, through faith – and this is not from yourselves, it is the gift of God.*

What makes John 1:14 unique is that the disclosure of grace and truth come through God's Anointed (the Messiah). Verses 1 through 18 of chapter 1 form the prologue to the gospel of John and parallel Genesis 1:1 – *In the beginning....* John 1:1 reads: *In the beginning was the Word....* The Holman Bible translates John 1:14 this way: *The Word became flesh and took up residence among us. We observed his glory as of the One and Only Son from the Father, full of grace and truth.*

God's grace and truth became visible in a person who "tabernacled among us," "pitched his tent among us" (literal meanings). In Jesus' words, life, and deeds we see grace and truth as we never could have imagined them. No longer was it words, it was encapsulated in a person. This is the most amazing miracle in all of Scripture. Grace and truth became first-hand and observable in the everyday world. That grace and truth knew no boundaries or limits. Barriers were broken, boundaries were crossed, the excluded were included, the outcasts were no longer ignored. Grace and the truth of God's love and forgiveness were seen, felt, and experienced as never before.

> In Luke 4:14-30, immediately following Jesus' "testing" in the wilderness, we find him ready to preach his first sermon in his hometown synagogue of Nazareth. As the guest rabbi for the day, he was handed the scroll of Isaiah and he found the text he wanted to use: it was all about good news to the poor, freedom for prisoners, sight for the blind, and freedom for the oppressed. As Messiah, he was announcing the inauguration of God's reign.[1]

We are told that the people were amazed at his gracious words. Here was a hometown boy, Joseph's son they murmured, making an unbelievable claim. The kicker came when he cited two prophets, Elijah and Elisha who reached out beyond Israel in their ministries to the widow Zarephath of Sidon and Naaman the Syrian (I Kings 17, 2 Kings 5). "The outsiders, the outcast, and even the Gen-

---

1   David L. Tiede, *Luke* (Minneapolis: Augsburg Publishing House, 1988), 104.

tiles receive the prophet and the benefits of God's reign ahead of the elect."[2] Jesus was indicating that he was going to continue the message and ministry of grace and truth beyond any idea of exclusiveness. In Luke's two-part story (Luke and Acts), he demonstrates the radical inclusion of all in the way he ends the book of Acts: *(Paul) proclaimed the kingdom of God and taught about the Lord Jesus Christ – with all boldness and WITHOUT HINDRANCE* (28:31, my emphasis). Luke's double volume ends with the announcement: "All grace and glory broke loose!"

Paul is unable to find words big enough to describe just how much grace he was preaching: Romans 5:15: *where sin abounded mercy abounded still more* (SCHONFIELD); *where sin has increased, grace has increased even* more (LATTIMORE). Sin can never be so great that God's grace is not greater still. The central message sounds shocking: you can't out-sin God's grace. God always has more grace than you have sin.

Ephesians 2:6-7 is the classic text on God's extravagance in his dispensing of grace: *the incomparable riches of his grace, expressed in his kindness to us in Christ Jesus* draws the biggest picture of grace I can find. Lattimore speaks of *the surpassing abundance of his grace.* This superabundance of God's grace is miraculous beyond measure when we discover that it cannot be earned, deserved, or purchased – it is pure gift. The final realization of this incredible truth set Martin Luther free. The bounty of grace is there, never to be exhausted. And it is ours for the receiving.

Ramifications

One Thing We Don't Have To Worry About.

> We're good at getting in the way. Perhaps we're afraid that if we move, God might use people and methods we don't approve of, that rules will be broken and theologies questioned.

---
2 Ibid, 109.

Perhaps we're afraid that if we get out of the way, this grace thing might get out of hand. Well, guess what? It already has. Grace got out of hand the moment the God of the universe hung on a Roman cross and with outstretched hands looked out upon those who had hung with him there and declared, "Father, forgive them, for they know not what they do."[3]

The grace and truth that John 1:14 declares entered the world in Jesus, was an overflowing grace and truth that was out of hand at the moment of the Incarnation. The devotional series from which I read each morning, has this prayer for the week: "Lord, I pray that your grace may always precede and follow me...."[4] I like to tell people who are struggling with difficulties: "Don't worry. God's got you hemmed in! He's got you hemmed in with his grace." To know that God's grace *precedes* and *follows* us is the assurance that nothing in the future can really get out of hand and nothing that haunts us from the past can really get out of hand because God's out of hand grace saturates all of our days.

Almost everyone's favorite hymn is Amazing Grace. My favorite line (from the original) is: *"Tis grace hath bro't me safe thus far, And grace will lead me home."* Grace is not only our traveling companion, grace is our escort. I'll never forget visiting with an elderly man in the hospital. He startled me with a direct question: "Do you think I'll go to heaven when I die?" I reflected a few moments and returned his question with one of my own: "Do you think I will go to heaven when I die?" He quickly answered, "Yes!" "Why do you believe that?" I asked. He paused and quietly responded: "I've heard enough of your sermons to know the answer to that question. It's because of grace." And he smiled because he had supplied the answer to his opening question.

We don't have to worry that, in an attempt to offer reconciliation, we are going into territory God has marked "off limits." The

---

3   Rachel Held Evans, *Searching for Sunday* (Nashville: Nelson Books, 2015), 39-40.
4   Phyllis Tickle, *The Divine Hours: Prayers for Autumn and Wintertime* (New York: Doubleday, 2000), 38.

one who came to live out God's grace and truth never saw any of those signs anywhere he went. Jesus never told anyone, "Because of the kind of life you have lived, you can't expect the full measure of God's grace. You're one of those who will get into the Kingdom by the 'skin of your teeth.'" The full measure of grace is the only degree of grace God ever offers. Jesus told a parable to underscore that very point; I used it as the basis for a sermon I called: "Upsetting Grace."

In Matthew 20, Jesus tells the story about the owner of a vineyard who went to the marketplace to hire some daily workers. He hired workers at 6:00 a.m., 9:00 a.m., noon, 3:00 p.m. and 5:00 p.m. The workday ended at 6:00 p.m. These workers were paid daily. There were many raised eyebrows when those who had been hired at 5:00 p.m. received a full day's wage. Those who were hired earlier expected to receive more but, they too, received a day's wage. They began to grumble against the landowner who responded, *"Friend, I am not being unfair to you. Didn't you agree to work for a denarius"* (the usual daily wage)? *Are you envious because I am generous?"* (Matthew 20:1-16).

This was only "upsetting grace" because someone else received what they didn't earn, what they didn't deserve. It is easily forgotten that grace is always a gift. It is never earned. It is never deserved. If we recognize ourselves as the recipients of this kind of grace, how can we ever grumble about God's treating others the way he has treated us? The realization that we have received this out-of-hand grace should make us grateful for God's generosity with all others who open their lives to receive it.

One of my favorite comic strips was by the late Doug Marlette. It was titled *Kudzu* but the star of the series was Rev. Will B. Dunn. Here is one of the classics:[5]

> In the first frame Rev. Will B. Dunn is kneeling, with folded hands, in prayer. In frame two he says: "Lord, I don't want a lot. All I ask for is my just desserts." In frame three a

---

5   Doug Marlette, *Just a Simple Country Preacher* (Nashville: Thomas Nelson Publishers, 1985), pages not numbered.

whipped-cream pie has smacked him in the face. In frame four he looks up and says, "Let me rephrase that."

Like any good parable, that one needs no unpacking.

A SURPRISING SIN

> *All the people said to Samuel, "Pray to the Lord your God for your servants, so that we may not die; for we have added to all our sins the evil of demanding a king for ourselves."...And Samuel said to the people,...far be it from me that I should sin against the Lord by ceasing to pray for you....*(I Samuel 12:19, 23, NRSV).

Why wouldn't Samuel pray for them? Wasn't he the great prophet in Israel? Wasn't that a part of his job? Well, something had happened that set this prophet off on the biggest fit he ever had. The people felt they needed a king in Israel and Samuel kept telling them they already had a king, a divine king, the Lord himself. But that wasn't enough for the people. They wanted a king like every other nation had. So, God chose one for them and told Samuel to anoint him. Samuel anointed Saul as the first king of the nation of Israel but he wasn't happy about it. He never did get happy about it. He felt the people had sinned against God by demanding a king. Samuel felt the people had rejected God and they had rejected him as God's chief spokesperson. The people were fearful that this great prophet would stop praying for them now that they had a king. He said it would be a sin not to pray for them.

The basis on which Samuel prays for the people is the basis on which we can always pray for others. Samuel tells the people: *"Do not be afraid; you have done all this evil...(But) the Lord will not cast away his people, for his great name's sake, because it has pleased the Lord to make you a people for himself"* (I Samuel 12:20, 22, NRSV). Samuel prays on the basis of who God is, not on the basis of who they are or who he is. The promised praying in our text comes the only way it can ever come: not on the basis of a people who have sinned or a prophet who is out of sorts, but on the basis of the God who is the same yesterday, today, and forever in his grace, mercy, and compassion. He prays on the basis of HIS NAME'S SAKE (*name* being the essence of who God is).

Hit 'Em One For The Lord!

William Willimon always has a way of presenting the Gospel in fresh ways. For example:

> It seems to me that the Bible says that true conversion… comes at the point when a person realizes that the God who was once considered to be a powerful enemy, who was to be avoided or bargained with is, in reality a friend who is to be trusted. Just when we expect to get clobbered for our guilt, we get clobbered by grace.[6]

My suggestion (for myself as well!) is when you want to "Hit someone for the Lord!" (if that is even possible), instead, "Clobber them with grace!" Everyone will be surprised and the possibilities for transformation are endless. Willimon explains in further detail a large part of what that clobbering involves:

> We are so preoccupied with the need to 'make a decision for Christ' that we forget that, in Christ, God has once and for all made a decision for us! In getting down on our knees to 'accept Christ,' we overlook the fact that if the life and death of Jesus Christ means anything, they mean that God accepts us! You and I can do little to add to or to improve upon God's acceptance of us in Christ expect to say yes to it and enjoy it.[7]

Concluding Thoughts

The book of Lamentations has no title in Hebrew. Like the first five books in the Old Testament, it was known by the first word in the text, the word "how." There is an amazing discovery to be made in the book of "*How!*" You really don't expect to find

---

6 William Willimon, *The Gospel for the Person Who Has Everything* (Valley Forge: Judson Press, 1984), 25.
7 Ibid.

much inspiration from a book titled *Lamentations,* which is a poem commemorating the destruction of Jerusalem by the Babylonians in 586 B.C. Tucked into the following verses is the inspiration for a traditional hymn:

> *The thought of my affliction and my homelessness is wormwood and gall! My soul continually thinks of it and is bowed down within me. But this I call to mind, and therefore I have hope: The steadfast love of the Lord never ceases, his mercies never come to an end; they are new every morning: great is your faithfulness. "The Lord is my portion," says my soul, "therefore I will hope in him."* (Lamentations 3:19-24, NRSV).

From the Celebrating Grace Hymnal [8] here is the first verse and chorus of "Great Is Thy Faithfulness":

Great is Thy faithfulness, O God, my Father,
there is no shadow of turning with Thee;
Thou changest not, Thy compassions they fail not;
as thou hast been, Thou forever wilt be.
Great is Thy faithfulness! Great is Thy faithfulness!
Morning by morning new mercies I see;
all I have needed, Thy hand hath provided;
great is Thy faithfulness, Lord, unto me.

---

8   *Celebrating Grace Hymnal* (Macon Celebrating Grace, Inc., 2010), 48.

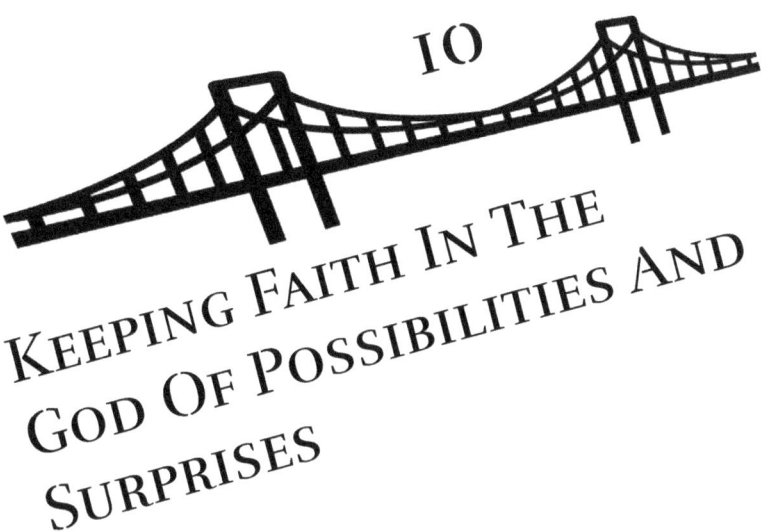

10
Keeping Faith In The God Of Possibilities And Surprises

Biblical Soundings

John 4:7 – *When a Samaritan woman came to draw water, Jesus said to her, "Will you give me a drink?"*

Genesis 18:13 – *Then the Lord said to Abraham, "Why did Sarah laugh and say, 'Will I really have a child, now that I am old?' Is anything too hard for the Lord?"*

Acts 28:30-31 – *For two whole years Paul stayed there in his own rented house and welcomed all who came to see him. He proclaimed the kingdom of God and taught about the Lord Jesus Christ – with all boldness and without hindrance!* (Literally: unhindered).

Genesis 33:1-4 – *Jacob looked up and there was Esau, coming with his four hundred men: so he divided the children among Leah, Rachel and the two female servants. He put the female servants and their children in the front, Leah and her children next, and Rachel and Joseph in the rear. He himself went on ahead and bowed down to the ground seven times as he approached his brother.*

But Esau ran to meet Jacob and embraced him; he threw his arms around his neck and kissed him. And they wept,.

Matthew 1:1, 3, 5, 6: *This is the genealogy of Jesus the Messiah the Son of David, the son of Abraham: Judah the father of Perez and Zerah whose mother was Tamar,...Salmon the father of Boaz, whose mother was Rahab, Boaz the father of Obed, whose mother was Ruth,...David was the father of Solomon, whose mother had been Uriah's wife.*

SURPRISE! SURPRISE! SURPRISE!

Just then his disciples returned and were surprised to find him talking with a woman (John 4:27). The word translated *surprise* doesn't begin to capture other meanings of the Greek word: *At this his students came and were amazed that he was talking with a woman* (BARNSTONE); *At this juncture his disciples returned, and were dumbfounded to find him talking with a woman* (SCHONFIELD).

Unfortunately, we have so tamed the Gospels with our repeated readings, that we have let the extraordinary fall victim to the ordinary. In the first written Gospel (Mark), the response of the crowd to Jesus' forgiving and healing of a paralyzed man sets the theme of surprise: *This amazed everyone and they praised God, saying, "We have never seen anything like this!"* (Mark 2:12). Barnstone translates that *all were astonished* and Schonfield translates that *they were all astounded.*

For those who believed Jesus of Nazareth was the long-awaited Messiah, the agenda they envisioned for the Anointed One had to be completely rewritten. If we were able to read the Gospels with fresh eyes and listening ears, we would be surprised at how many upset apple carts would litter our theological landscape. Even John the baptizer (literally, "the dipper") was so caught off guard that, from prison, he sent his disciples with a question for Jesus: "*Are you the one who was to come, or should we expect someone else?*" (Matthew 11:3). Jesus' response to that question is a directive to all of us: "*Go back and report to John what you hear and see....*" (11:4).

If we listen to what Jesus says and look carefully at what he does, we come to only one conclusion about his role as Messiah:

"Surprise! Surprise! Surprise!" We should come to expect the unexpected and exchange impossible for possible. Perhaps that's why true conversion is likened to being born from above – it is not achieved by common earthly sense (whatever that might mean).

WHAT ABOUT THESE IMPOSSIBLE POSSIBILITIES?

Laughter seems the most appropriate response to God's assurance that Abraham and Sarah will have a son who will be the promise-bearer. Old age has carried them both well beyond the child-bearing years. When God assures Abraham that age will not be a barrier to his promise, Abraham falls facedown and laughs (Genesis 17:17). Later, three visitors show up and repeat the promise of a son. Sarah is listening at the entrance to the tent and laughs to herself. In Genesis 18:13 we read: *But the Lord said to Abraham, "Why did Sarah laugh?"* This amazing identification of one of the three as "the Lord" and the charge against Sarah are puzzling. It all seems so obvious to the casual reader. Sarah denies laughing, but the Lord corrects her: "*Yes, you did laugh*" (Genesis 18:15).

Surprises and impossible possibilities appear to suggest that God may be in the laughter business. He tells Abraham (17:19) that the promised son is to be called Isaac; Isaac means *he laughs*. When Isaac is born, Sarah declares, "*God has brought me laughter, and everyone who hears about this will laugh with me.*" Abraham laughs, then Sarah laughs, and God's response is to laugh with them.

WHO WOULD HAVE THOUGHT IT POSSIBLE?

When the Luke-Acts saga ends, the gospel message has spread from Jerusalem to Rome. Not only has it spread, but the adverb with which Acts concludes is hidden in the translation with which most of us grew up (KJV): *Paul dwelt two whole years in his own hired house, and received all that came in unto him, preaching the kingdom of God, and teaching those things which concern the Lord Jesus Christ, with all confidence, no man forbidding him* (28:30-31). The best translation of the final Greek word in Acts is unhindered.

The TNIV provides the amazement that this word conveys: *(Paul) proclaimed the kingdom of God and taught about the Lord Jesus Christ – with all boldness and without hindrance!* No wonder the book of Acts concludes with an exclamation!

IT IS SO UNLIKELY THAT WE NEVER SAW IT COMING.

One of the most famous of all the family stories in Genesis is Jacob's stealing of Esau's blessing (Genesis 27). As the firstborn, the covenant blessing was a given. With the help of his mother, Rebecca, Jacob decides it will be an easy matter to trick his blind father into giving that blessing to him. Unfortunately, we lack the context in which to fully understand all that is going on. We do know that Esau is a "man's man" who is the father's favorite and Jacob is a more at-home son: contemplative, and devious (sorry for the judgment). When a famished Esau trades his first-born right for a bowl of "that red stuff" (literal meaning), I don't believe he had any idea what he was doing. The result of the trickery is that Jacob is forced to flee from the wrath of his brother and Rebecca never sees her favorite son again.

Some twenty-odd years later, when Jacob returns from Paddan Aram, he is rich in wives, children, and possessions. Jacob sends messengers ahead to let Esau know he is coming and is alarmed to learn that Esau is coming to meet him – with four hundred men. The red flags go up and sins of the past come rushing to his mind, He splits the caravan into two divisions and makes certain Esau receives a treasure-trove of gifts before he meets any of them. A sleepless night results in a wrestling match (with God and with himself). This contest results in a limp and a new name: Israel. The next morning, he is ready to meet his brother as a different person. He has no idea that Esau has also become a different person.

Jacob bows down seven times before his brother (in repentance?). Esau responds by running to meet him, throwing his arms around him, and kissing him. Then they both weep (Genesis 33:3-4). Jacob learns that Esau has been blessed after all with so much that in response to Jacob's offer of gifts he says, *"I already have plenty!"* (33:9). This is an indication of a remarkable change in Esau (and in Jacob). Another of God's amazing surprises is recorded in a single sentence. The background for that sentence is Jacob's analysis of the wrestling match: *So Jacob called the place Peniel, saying, "It is because I saw God face to face, and yet my life was spared"* (Genesis 32:30). After his meeting with Esau, he tells him: *"To see your face is like seeing the face of God, now that you have received me favorably"* (33:10). That is more than a fairy tale ending. The brother who couldn't receive a blessing from his father gave Jacob a blessing he never saw coming.

AN UNIMAGINABLE FAMILY TREE

It's given so casually that it is easy to miss the explosive nature of the revelations. In Jesus' ministry, he never encountered anyone who was to be written off. Nothing was a barrier to their having a place at the table in God's Kingdom. In Matthew's genealogy of Jesus, we find some highly unlikely names: Tamar, Rahab, Ruth, and Bathsheba (referred to as Uriah's wife). Tamar disguised herself with the veil of a temple prostitute and seduced Judah; Rahab was a prostitute in Jericho who hid the spies of Joshua in her house; Ruth was a Moabite; and Bathsheba was David's wife as the result of adultery and murder. William Barclay provides this summary:

> If Matthew had ransacked the pages of the Old Testament for improbable candidates, he could not have discovered four more incredible ancestors for Jesus Christ. But, surely, there is something very lovely here. Here, at the very beginning of his gospel, Matthew shows us in symbol the very essence of the gospel of God in Jesus Christ, for here he shows us the barriers going down.[1]

---

1   William Barclay, *Matthew*, Vol. 1, 7.

Ramifications

Are Things More Open Than We Have Imagined?

The shock value of Deuteronomy 9:13-14 is enough for weeks of discussion and dialogue. Moses tells the people what God said to him: "*I have seen that this people is indeed a stubborn people. Let me alone that I may destroy them and blot out their name from under heaven; and I will make of you a nation mightier and more numerous than they*" (NRSV). A man of lesser status might have said, "Right on, Lord! This is certainly a bunch of no-goods. I'm sick and tired of them myself. Starting over again with me and my family will probably produce better results in the long run." But this is not what Moses said. Moses does not let God alone. For forty days and nights, he fasted and prayed for the people. After God said, "*Let me alone,*" and Moses didn't do it, we then read the testimony of Moses as to what happened: "*But the Lord listened to me….*" (Deut. 9:19). As a result of God's listening to Moses, the people were spared. That's not all. "*The Lord was so angry with Aaron that he was ready to destroy him, but I interceded also on behalf of Aaron at the same time*" (Deuteronomy 9:20, NRSV).

Moses was a great advocate, a great intercessor, a great bridge builder. Moses spoke with God on behalf of others, God heard, and things changed. Twice in the book of Amos (7:3 and 7:6), as a result of the prayers of the prophet, we are told that *the Lord relented concerning this*….(NRSV). Those who believe that God's will is unchangeable, either skip over verses like this or explain them as meaning something other than the clear indication of the text. Here is the startling word from Exodus 32:14: *And the Lord repented of the evil which he thought to do to his people* (NRSV). We usually use the word repent to meaning feeling sorry for something. The true biblical meaning of the word has to do with a new direction. When the Bible tells us that God repents, it simply means that he wills a change. And things change when advocates, intercessors, and bridge builders pray.

What About "The Whoosh"?

> In his essay "Is That All There Is?" Harvard professor James Wood discusses Charles Taylor's description of "fullness." Sometimes one experiences a fullness in which the world suddenly seems charged with meaning, coherence, and beauty that break through our ordinary sense of being in the world. Some who experience and know unavoidably that there is infinitely more to life than just physical health, wealth, and freedom. There is depth and wonder and some kind of Presence beyond ordinary life. Philosophers Hubert Dreyfus and Sean Kelly call the experience "The Whoosh."[2]

I believe that "Whoosh" is experienced from the God of possibilities and surprises because I believe what David Tracy writes: "Although God is usually read as a noun, the name should be read as a verb."[3] The Hebrews did not sit and contemplate the "nature" of God and then write a description of his attributes. They believed they had encountered God in their lives and in their history. In biblical times, most gods were considered to be local deities and when one traveled to another town it was necessary to change gods. That is one of the reasons Jacob was so taken aback that, when he awoke from his dream at Bethel, he declared, *"Surely the Lord is in this place, and I was not aware of it"* (Genesis 28:16). Jacob had not left God behind in Beersheba with his father Isaac. God is the God of possibilities and surprises throughout the Old Testament. He is active in the life of his people and his world on every page. That's how the Hebrews came to understand God – through the ways they believed he had encountered them and worked in their lives.

In the sequel to David Heller's *Dear God, What Religion Were the Dinosaurs?*, Marti, age 10, writes: "Who are you? How can we find you? You sure are difficult to pin down."[4] My answer to Marti would be, "If you can pin down God, he isn't God. He is the God

---

2   Timothy Keller, *Making Sense of God*, 18.
3   David Tracy, *Fragments*, 12.
4   David Heller, *Dear God: What Religion Were the Dinosaurs?*, 111.

of your making." Of course, that is the same problem the Hebrews had: they couldn't pin down God. He was always showing up in unlikely places to unlikely people and making unlikely promises along with unlikely demands. Jacob was surprised that God showed up at Bethel; that was not all of the surprise. He probably expected a lecture on respect, honoring your father, and fair treatment for your brother. God could have said a great many things, but instead, he surprised Jacob with an unbelievable word of grace:

> *"I am the Lord, the God of your father Abraham and the God of Isaac. I will give you and your descendants the land on which you are lying. Your descendants will be like the dust of the earth, and you will spread out to the west and to the east, to the north and to the south. All peoples on earth will be blessed through you and your offspring. I am with you and will watch over you wherever you go, and I will bring you back to this land. I will not leave you until I have done what I have promised you."* (Genesis 28:13-15).

God tells Jacob what we all need to hear because most of us are afraid of something, have issues of insecurity about things, and are on the run from something or someone who is threatening us in some way. The message to Jacob is God's message to all of us: "*I am with you…I will not leave you.*" (That is the same word we hear from Jesus in Matthew 28:20 which I like to call "The Great Promise.": *And remember, I am with you always, to the end of the age"* HOLMAN). I think we, too, are surprised by the God who says to us: "I will be with you; I will not leave you."

ANGEL UNAWARE?

One of my boyhood heroes was Roy Rogers and I had never missed one of his films at the weekly Saturday matinees. One of the most inspiring stories to come from the life of Rogers and his wife, Dale Evans Rogers, involved their daughter Robin. She was born with Downs Syndrome and heart problems. After her death, Dale Evans wrote the book *Angel Unaware* about how this child had changed the faith and lives of her parents. She became a blessing with a capital "B."

I almost wanted to use the same phrase to describe Mattie J. T. Stepanek. He died at age 13 (July 17, 1990 – June 22, 2004) from dysautonomic mitochondrial myopathy, a neuromuscular disease. Wikipedia gives this overview of the boy who was a poet from age 3.

> He wanted to be remembered as "a poet, a peacemaker, and a philosopher who played." He published seven best-selling books of poetry and peace essays. Before his death at the age of 13, he had become known as a peace advocate and motivational speaker.

From the book *Reflections of a Peacemaker: A Portrait Through Heartsongs* (what Mattie called his poems),[5] I have chosen two of his heartsongs to indicate the unbelievable perception and spirituality of this young man. I begin with an incredible testimony from his mother, Jeni Stepanek:

> Considering all the challenges, all the losses, all the unknowns, all the ongoing emotional and physical pain that was part of Mattie's entire life, it is amazing that he was such an optimistic, inspiring, confident, and genuinely happy human being. When he was in kindergarten, a television reporter was interviewing him about his first poetry book, *Heartsongs*, which he had submitted for a countywide contest in the public school system. I was sitting in the next room and overheard her ask my five-year-old child, "So, Mattie, do you have a philosophy for your life?"
>
> Chuckling to myself, I wondered why an adult would even think that such a young child would know what the word "philosophy" meant, much less have contemplated a guiding principle for his personal life. To my astonishment, Mattie answered her without hesitation, "Oh, yes, ma'am. My philosophy is 'always remember to play after every storm.' And he proceeded to explain to her what he meant by the various

---

5   Mattie J. Stepanek, *Reflections of a Peacemaker* (Kansas City: Andrews McMeel Publishing, 2005).

"storms" we encounter in life, and the important matter of "playing" as a source of celebration, rejuvenation, and appreciation."[6]

Here are two of Mattie's heartsongs; the first is from Thanksgiving Prayer:[7]

> Dear God,
> Let us be truly thankful
>   For the gift of each new day.
>   Help us to live thankfully throughout the year,
>   So that when our time comes for the gift of Eternity,
>   The eternal echo of our life here on earth
>   Will be a song of goodness worth remembering.
> (Written when Mattie was ten years old.)

Here is Mattie's Recipe for Peace (I call it the recipe for bridge-building). It was written when he was eleven:[8]

> Peace is possible.
> Make peace an attitude.
> Want it.
> Make peace a habit.
> Live it.
> Make peace a reality,
> Share it.
> Peace is possible.
> Make peace matter.
> Make peace a priority.
> Our priority.
> Make peace a choice.
> Our choice.
> Peace is possible.
> We must

---

6   Ibid, 112.
7   Ibid, 74.
8   Ibid, 177

Think gently,
Speak gently,
Live gently,
Peace is possible.
Be happy with who you are.
Be happy with who others are.
Be happy that we are.
Peace is possible.
Role model acceptance.
Love others.
Role model forgiveness.
Encourage others
Role model tolerance.
Treasure others.
Peace is possible.
Peace is possible.
Peace is possible.

If you want a book that will inspire, motivate, challenge, and encourage you to give life your best, get this book and keep it close. It beats any "breaking news" any day! You will discover in these writings the truth of what former President Jimmy Carter wrote: "My wife and I have been to more than 120 nations. And we have known kings and queens, and we've known presidents and prime ministers, but the most extraordinary person whom I have ever known in my life is Mattie Stepanek."[9]

Concluding Thoughts

Pope Francis has summarized for me the basis on which I believe in the God of possibilities and surprises: "There is no corner of our heart that God's love cannot reach."[10] I believe this is possible because of the most surprising thing God ever did.

---

9   Ibid., back cover.
10 Pope Francis, *Happiness in This Life* (New York: Random House, 2017), 177.

There is a bit of irony here: I wanted to make Jesus "relevant" to nonbelievers by showing that he could fix all their problems and heal their brokenness (which is obviously important), but I completely missed the fact that divinity clothing himself in humanity is itself the most relevant thing God could have done. In short, the whole reason God can help you with the day-to-day difficulties of life is because he is invested in earth and in humanity, so much so that he entered into these realities in Christ."[11]

The Gospel story really has two large miracle bookends: the Incarnation and the Resurrection. These two surprising, and only possible for God, actions are the two most important events in the New Testament. Everything hangs on these two manifestations of God's love, mercy, and grace. And they keep alive the word "possibilities."

I recently rewatched "*The Finest Hours*" on DVD. The subtitle is: "The Impossible Rescue." It is the true story of an incredible rescue operation, A massive record-storm struck off the coast of Cape Cod and on February 18, 1952, Barnie Webber with a crew of three set out to rescue men trapped on the SS Pendleton oil Tanker which had broken in two. Some of the Coast Guard members refused to go out in the storm in such a small boat. The waves were forty to sixty feet high. The rescue boat was a small twelve-seater. Shortly after departure from Chatham, Massachusetts, a huge wave tore the compass from its mount and swept it overboard leaving nothing to guide the rescue boat except the searchlight.

It went down in history as one of the most daring rescue attempts. Thirty-two survivors and four crew fit into a lifeboat built for twelve, thirty-six men in a thirty-six-foot boat. Bernie Webber decided not to wear a life jacket in order to give him the best maneuverability to control the boat. In one of the documentaries on the DVD, Barnie Webber's daughter reports that her father said he felt the boat surrounded by supernatural forces and felt the

---

11   Jason J. Stellman, *Misfit Faith* (New York: Convergent, 2017).

Lord's hand on his shoulder. I believe it was the hand of the God of impossible possibilities.

CONCLUSION

THE GREAT AND FINAL RECONCILIATION

Revelation 21:1-5 — *Then I saw "a new heaven and a new earth," for the first heaven and the first earth had passed away, and there was no longer any sea. I saw the Holy City, the new Jerusalem, coming down out of heaven from God, prepared as a bride beautifully dressed for her husband. And I heard a loud voice from the throne saying, "Look! God's dwelling place is now among his people, and he will dwell with them. They will be his people, and God himself will be with them and be their God. He will wipe every tear from their eyes, There will be no more death or mourning or crying or pain, for the old order of things has passed away." He who was seated on the throne said, "I am making everything new!"*

"Although I have long-run hopes for a much better world, I am not looking for utopia, certainly not in the short run. I'd settle for sanity."[1] Right now, it looks as though even sanity is in short supply. That is the reason for this book and the plea for claiming our forgotten calling to work in the same kind of world in which Jesus and Paul did their ministries. The text from Revelation lets us know when sanity is coming: with the new heaven and the new earth and God dwelling with his people in the restored relationship of the long-lost Eden. Speculation about that great and final reconciliation runs the gamut, but a few samples give helpful perspectives:

1   Steven Klees, *The Conscience of a Conservative*, 157.

Jack Boughton says he has more ideas about heaven every day. He said, "Mainly I just think about the splendors of the world and multiply by two. I'd multiply by ten or twelve if I had the energy. But two is much more than sufficient for my purposes."[2]

At a particular moment Jesus came into the world. And as some particular hour when we least expect, a veil will be lifted and there will be an ending and a beginning, creation purged, healed, and renewed, afterward forever in a new and right relationship to God, who so loves the world. The clocks will stop, and we will find ourselves on the threshold of eternity.

Speculation about the afterlife has a long history....How can the dead live again? We will see. Why should they live again, motley and cantankerous as they have been for the most part? Because God values them. And he is the God not of the dead but of the living.[3]

According to an old medieval legend, the Apostles assembled together in heaven to recelebrate the Last Supper. There was one place vacant, until through the door Judas came in and Christ rose and kissed him and said, "We have waited for you."[4]

Revelation 21:5: *He who was seated on the throne said, "I am making everything new!" Then he said, "Write this down, for these words are trustworthy and true." (TNIV).* N.T. Wright makes this comment on the verse: "Although God promises to come and make everything new, that newness is still a mystery full of surprises."[5]

---

2 Marilynne Robinson, *Gilead* (London: Vigero Press, 2020), 167.
3 Marilynne Robinson, *The Givenness of Things* (New York: Farrar, Straus and Giroux, 2015), 237, 239.
4 Simon Wisenthal, *The Sunflower* (New York: Shocken Books, 1998),108.
5 Dallas Willard, et al., *Faith That Matters,* 232.

Bibliography Of Quoted Sources

Barclay, William. *The Daily Study Bible: The Gospel of Luke*. Philadelphia: The Westminster Press, 1956.

———. *The Daily Study Bible: The Gospel of Matthew*, Volume 1.
Philadelphia: The Westminster Press, 1958.

Barnstone, William. *The New Covenant*, Vol 1. New York: Riverhead Books, 2002.

———. *Restored New Testament*. New York: W. W. Norton & Company, 2009.

Beard, Alex. *Natural Born Learners*. London: Weidenfeld & Nicolson, 2018.

Bobrick, Benson. *Wide as the Waters*. New York: Simon & Schuster, 2001.

Box, C. J. *Paradise Valley*. New York: Minotaur Books, 2018, 281.

Buechner, Frederick, et al. *Faith That Matters*. New York: HyperOne, 2018.

Campolo, Tony and Bart. *Things We Wish We Had Said*. Dallas: Word Incorporated, 1989.

Carter-Scott, Cherie. *If Life is a Game… These Are the Rules.* Naperville, IL: Simple Truths, 1998.

Celebrating Grace Hymnal. Macon: Celebrating Grace, Inc., 2010.

Coe, Alexis. *You Never Forget Your First.* New York: Penguin Books, 2020.

Collins, Paul. *Sixpence House.* New York: Bloomsbury, 2003.

Covey, Stephen R. *The 7 Habits of Highly Effective People.* New York: Simon and Schuster, 1989.

Crichton, Michael. *Jurassic Park.* New York: Alfred A. Knopf, 1990.

Davids, Peter. *Commentary on James: New International Greek Testament Commentary.* Grand Rapids: Wm. B. Eerdmans Publishing Co., 1983.

Drury, Bob and Clavin, Tom. *Valley Forge.* New York: Simon & Schuster, 2018.

Evans, Rachel Held. *Inspired.* New York: Nelson Books, 2018.

_____. *Searching for Sunday.* Nashville: Nelson Books, 2015.

Fowler, James. Stages of Faith. New York: HarperOne, 1981.

Fox, Michael J. *No Time Like the Future.* New York: Flatiron Books, 2020.

Francis, Pope. *Happiness in This Life.* New York: Random House, 2017.

Gaebelein, Frank E., ed. *The Expositor's Bible Commentary, Volume 2.* Grand Rapids: Zondervan, 1990.

_____. *The Expositor's Bible Commentary, Volume 8.* Grand Rapids: Zondervan, 1984.

_____. *The Expositor's Bible Commentary, Volume 10.* Grand Rapids: Zondervan, 1976.

Gosling, Emily. *Great Minds Don't Think Alike.* London: ILEX, 2018.

Grant, Adam. *Think Again.* New York: Viking, 2021.

Hare, Douglas R. A. *Matthew: Interpretation.* Louisville: John Knox Press, 1993.
Hart, David Bentley. *Atheist Delusions.* New Haven: Yale University Press, 2009.
Hauerwas, Stanley. *Matthew.* Grand Rapids: Brazos Press, 2006.
Heller, David. *Dear God: What Religion Were the Dinosaurs?* New York: Doubleday, 1990.
Higdon, Ronald. *All I Need to Know I'm Still Learning At 80.* Gonzalez, FL: Energion Publications, 2017.
Johnson, Paul. *Jesus: A Biographer from a Believer.* New York: Viking, 2010.
Keller, Timothy. *Making Sense of God.* New York: Viking, 2016.
Kelly, Matthew. *Rediscover the Saints.* North Palm Beach: Blue Sparrow, 2019.
Kelsey, Morton. *Companions on the Inner Way.* New York: Crossroad, 1983.
Klees, Steven. *The Conscience of a Progressive.* Winchester, UK: Zero Books, 2020.
Krznaric, Roman. *Carpe Diem Regained.* London: Unbound, 2017.
Kushner, Harold. *Nine Things I've Learned About Life.* New York: Anchor Books, 2015.
Marlette, Doug. *Just a Simple Country Preacher.* Nashville: Thomas Nelson Publishers, 1985.
McRaney, David. *You Are Now Less Dumb.* New York: Gotham Books, 2013.
Merton, Thomas. *Passion for Peace.* New York: Crossroad, 1996.
Oates, Wayne. *The Struggle to be Free.* Philadelphia: Westminster Press, 1983.
Odell, Jenny. *How To Do Nothing.* Brooklyn: Melville House, 2019.
Phillips, Emo. *GQ,* June, 1999.

Raeper, William and Edwards, Linda. *Brief Guide to Ideas*. Grand Rapids: Zondervan, 1997.

Robinson, Marilynne. *Gilead*. London: Vigero Press, 2020.

_____. *The Givenness of Things*. New York: Farrar, Straus and Giroux, 2015.

Rohr, Richard. *The Universal Christ*. New York: Convergent, 2019.

Shirley, Craig. *Mary Ball Washington*. New York: Harper, 2019.

Stepanek, Mattie J. *Reflections of a Peacemaker*. Kansas City: Andrews McMeel Publishing, 2005.

St. John, Bob. *Landry: the Legend and the Legacy*. Nashville: Word Publishing, 2000.

Stellman, Jason J. *Misfit Faith*. New York: Convergent, 2017.

Sweet, Leonard I. *New Life in the Spirit*. Philadelphia: The Westminster Press, 1982.

Tickle, Phyllis. *The Divine Hours: Prayers for Autumn and Wintertime*. New York: Doubleday, 2000.

Tiede, David L. *Luke*. Minneapolis: Augsburg Publishing House, 1988.

Tracy, David. *Filaments*. Chicago: The University of Chicago Press, 2020.

_____. *Fragments*. Chicago: The University of Chicago Press, 2020.

Watson, Jimmy R. *Jesus is Still Speaking Through the Gospel of Mark*. Bloomington: Xlibris, 2011.

Weiner, Eric. *Man Seeks God*. New York: Twelve, 2011.

Willard, Dallas et al. *Faith That Matters*. New York: HarperOne, 2018.

Willimon, William. *The Gospel for the Person Who Has Everything*. Valley Forge: Judson Press, 1984.

Wisenthal, Simon. *The Sunflower*. New York: Shocken Books, 1998.

Wuest, Kenneth S. *Romans.* Grand Rapids: Wm. B. Eerdmans Publishing Company, 1955.

www.ingramcontent.com/pod-product-compliance
Lightning Source LLC
LaVergne TN
LVHW041630070426
835507LV00008B/542